EL TIANTE

Books by Joe Fitzgerald

EL TIANTE

THAT CHAMPIONSHIP FEELING

THE NEW ENGLAND PATRIOTS:
Minutemen of the Gridiron

EL TIANTE

The Luis Tiant Story

by Luis Tiant and Joe Fitzgerald

Doubleday & Company, Inc.   Garden City, New York   1976

ISBN: 0-385-12116-4
Library of Congress Catalog Card Number 76–2226
Copyright © 1976 by Luis Tiant and Joe Fitzgerald
All Rights Reserved
Printed in the United States of America
First Edition

Photos courtesy of the Boston *Globe,* The Personal Collection of Luis Tiant, Fred Keenan, Pam Schuyler, D. Finn, Ted Gartland and the Boston Red Sox.

TO MICHAEL JOSEPH FITZGERALD

For all of their courtesies and assistance, the author wishes to thank: Bill Crowley and Dick Bresciani of the Boston Red Sox; Tom Mee of the Minnesota Twins; Miss Rosemary O'Connor of the Cleveland Indians; Ernie Roberts and George Collins of the Boston *Globe;* Myer Ostroff and Ted Gartland of the Boston *Herald American;* Russ Schneider and Norty Friedrick of the Cleveland *Plain Dealer;* Miss Doris Skalstad of the Minneapolis Public Library; Miss Debbie Matheny of Bell & Howell (Ohio); Jerry Buckley; Fred Keenan; Pam Schuyler; Dick Raphael; Felix Fernandez; Jose Salazar; John Alevizos; editor Larry Jordan at Doubleday; and, personally, RQC.

Contents

Foreword

This book, and perhaps this man, arrives on the scene about one generation too late, for the age of sophistication is now upon us and we're told that people like Luis Tiant don't exist anymore, or if they do they're destined to get lost in the shuffle of people who *know where it's at.*

Once upon a time, before it became fashionable to rush into print with titillating tales of off-the-field activities, before selling out friendships for a quick buck became the literary vogue, before it was discovered that roguishness could be much more profitable than professionalism, the typical sports book portrayed its central figure as a paragon of virtue, as the embodiment of all that was good and decent and worthy of emulation.

That, of course, was bunk, and perhaps it's what led the pendulum to swing so far the other way, until it seems we've become a nation of cynics.

Now when we talk about old-fashioned values like pride in one's work, love of one's family, faith in one's religion, loyalty to one's friends, belief in one's own abilities, we run the risk of encouraging scorn, because *everyone knows* that's not the way things go today, especially not in sports, where agents and egos and broken words and busted contracts are as commonplace as hits, runs and errors.

And so I wondered, as I researched Tiant's career and met with his friends and family: *Is this going to come off like a pile of schmaltz, or will its credibility be sustained from beginning to end?*

I'll confess that bothered me, for the more I dug, the more incredible this man and his story seemed to be. Can a man endure enormous personal suffering and still be known to his friends as the funniest guy they've ever met? Can he be summarily discarded and rejected by one of the most competitive industries in America, only to fight his way back to the very peak of that profession?

Well, Luis Tiant has traveled that road, and the decision here was to record each and every step just the way it happened, according to the people who were there, because the deeper I got into this story, the more convinced I became that it's a story that *should be told* today, exactly the way it was, with no embellishments, no window dressings, no exaggerations.

Luis Tiant, it says here, is proof that the old-fashioned values *do* have their place in 1976, that it's still possible for a guy to beat back the odds by simple perseverance.

Maybe that sounds like a pail of hogwash, but be advised that you're going to find that sentiment recurring throughout the pages that follow. In every place he's played, and with everyone who's been along for part of the ride, the impressions were consistent.

Long after his baseball victories have been reduced to nostalgia and trivia, his personal victories will remain one of the nicest chapters in all of sports.

That's the way the pieces of this story came together, and that's the way the story will be told. Sophistication be damned! I think it's beautiful.

JOE FITZGERALD
January 5, 1976
Boston, Massachusetts

PART I
From Boyhood to Exile

CHAPTER 1

The King of el Remachado

The very first thought that rushed through young Luis Tiant's mind—even before the normal instinct to race for help—was the terrifying possibility that he had just killed Abelardo Aguiar.

For there was his 10-year-old friend, doubled over and retching, as his hands furiously rubbed that spot on his stomach where *la pelota* had struck him.

Aguiar, of course, should have known better. He had no one but himself to blame. Any kid in the neighborhood could have testified about the dangers of playing *el remachado* with Tiant. Spit into the wind and you get wet. Play *el remachado* with Tiant and you get hurt. It was more or less that basic, according to the kids who lived in Nicanor del Campo, a quiet, modest section of the Marianao district of Havana.

"When we were kids," recalls Juanito Quintana, a Delta employee in Tampa who fled Cuba in 1961, "we couldn't play too many ball games with Tiant because he was so much above average. I remember one time when I was eight and my father bought me a glove for Christmas. Tiant came over and we decided to throw a ball back and forth. He was only a year older than me, but I could never hold onto his throws. I kept pulling my glove off to blow cold air on my fingers. And it wasn't just me. It was that way with all of the kids we grew up with. In fact, I can remember kids who were older than Tiant who had trouble playing ball with him. That's how much better he was."

But the memories would fade with the stinging, and the next day usually found Juanito, Abelardo, Jorgito Raspall and the rest of that boyhood fraternity gathered on some nearby patch of grass, ready to engage Tiant—they always called him by his surname—in another round of *el remachado*.

"There were two ways to play the game," according to Raspall, who also left his homeland in 1961 and now works in Boston as a TWA official. "Everyone would be given a number. Then someone would throw the ball up into the air and yell out one of the numbers. If yours was called, you caught the ball, then threw it at whoever you thought you could hit. In the other version, there were no numbers. Whoever caught the ball got to throw it at the others."

In the former version, it was generally considered poor strategy to call out Luis' number.

"Now that he's in the great leagues," Quintana smiles, "I guess we can understand it better. But back then it was hard to believe how hard Tiant could throw that thing. Nobody would get close to him."

It was not a game for the slow afoot. Once you were hit three times, you were obliged to stand in front of a wall and let the rest of the group each get to throw at you.

"That was punishment for not being quick enough," Raspall explained.

All in all, Abelardo—who wasn't the quickest kid on the block to start with—probably should have come up with another idea that day, rather than challenging Tiant to a two-man duel of *el remachado*.

"Abelardo had a banana plant in back of his house," Luis remembers, "so we decided to eat some of them before we began playing. I think Abelardo ate too many. The first time I hit him with the ball, he yelled and started puking bananas! I didn't know what to do. I thought I had killed him."

Luis paused at the memory, then added an unnecessary afterthought. "It's a bad game," he frowned.

A much more popular one was *el corcho,* perhaps because it so closely resembled baseball—the most popular sport in the country —or maybe because the equipment was easier to come by.

The ball, or *la pelota,* in *el remachado* was usually a makeshift creation.

"We weren't so poor we couldn't eat," Quintana says, "but often no one had any money to buy a real ball. So we'd find those square boxes that cigarettes came in, then stuff them full of rolled-up newspapers and maybe add a stone to give them weight. When you got hit by one of those, especially if Tiant threw it, you were going to be hurt."

But the principal supplies for *el corcho* were an ordinary bottle cork and an old broomstick handle.

"We'd go down to *la bodega*—the marketplace—and find piles of empty bottles with the corks still in them," Raspall said. "Sometimes we'd put nails inside the corks, then go home and steal a few Band-Aids to wrap around them. We used to have very good times with them."

Especially Luis.

"He was terrific with the damned cork, too," Quintana laughed. "He could hit that thing so far you wouldn't believe it."

Indeed, in games and sports Tiant appeared to have the Midas touch. When the friends got together to play cards, usually with baseball trading cards as the stakes, it was Tiant who generally went home with the biggest winnings. When they lined up their spinning tops for impromptu competitions, often with the understanding that the winner got to keep his victims' tops, it was Tiant who eventually amassed the largest collection. And when they formed a circle to shoot marbles, you can imagine whose collection abounded.

"He was good at everything he tried to do," Raspall remembers. "He must have owned 20,000 marbles. But you know what I remember most about him? If he saw that another kid felt bad after losing, especially if he knew the kid didn't own many marbles, he'd always say, 'Here, take these and go home happy!' And he'd give the kid 25 or so."

There was a certain simplicity, a certain gentleness about Tiant that endeared him to his friends, that served to disarm any peers who might otherwise have been tempted to resent his natural precocity.

"Though he wasn't much bigger than the rest of us," Quintana noted, "he was a lot stronger. And you know how it is with kids: the stronger ones sometimes like to abuse the weaker ones. Tiant could have done that too, but he wasn't that type of kid. I think he just took his abilities for granted and never thought too much about them. He was nice to everybody, and I know if you ask any of the kids who grew up with Luis what they remember about him, they'll tell you they loved him. He was a very good friend."

Luis was born on November 23, 1940, the only child of Luis and Isabel Tiant, which made him too young to remember very much about his father's career in baseball.

It was a void he shared with most of the world, however, at least that portion of the world beyond the shorelines of Cuba.

From 1926 through 1948, the senior Tiant reigned as one of Cuba's most celebrated athletes, a marvelously gifted left-handed pitcher whose exploits were as legendary among Cubans as Babe Ruth's feats were among Americans. But they were worlds apart in opportunities; namely, the black world and the white world.

Through the first four years of its existence, the National Basketball Association (originally known as the Basketball Association of America) excluded nonwhites from its rosters. Then Chuck Cooper joined the Boston Celtics in 1950, opening the door for a veritable pantheon of outstanding stars like Bill Russell, Oscar Robertson and Elgin Baylor. Think of basketball without them.

For fifteen years no blacks could be found on National Football League rosters. Then halfback Kenny Washington, the great UCLA All-American, joined the Los Angeles Rams, paving the way for latter-day greats like Jimmy Brown, Gale Sayers and O. J. Simpson. Think of football without them.

But try to imagine baseball without Satchel Paige and Josh Gibson and Cool Papa Bell, and you'll find it isn't difficult because—unlike the other stars previously mentioned—these men, and scores of others like them, including Tiant, had the misfortune to be born too soon, to have spent the strength of their youth in near oblivion. The enormity of that loss continues to haunt major league baseball today.

Jackie Robinson ended the "gentlemen's agreement" that precluded blacks from big league rosters when Branch Rickey brought him to Brooklyn in 1947. By then, however, Tiant was 41 years old.

And, oh, what baseball fans had missed.

"There is absolutely no question about it," insists Monte Irvin, an assistant to Commissioner Bowie Kuhn. "He would have been a great, great star. What a pitcher! He had a great fastball and a screwball, and no one could mix pitches any better than he did. He knew how to pitch. And he had one of the best moves toward first base that I've ever seen in a lifetime in this game."

According to one anecdote, which Irvin and others are quick to confirm, Tiant's pickoff move once resulted in a remarkable mixup play. With runners on first and third and one man out, Tiant went into his pirouette motion. His leg went up, he teetered and tottered, his head bobbed and danced, and then he fired a bullet to first.

"The batter was so confused he swung for strike three," Irvin laughed. "And the man on first was out, too. The funniest part of it all was that the batter started insisting he had fouled off the pitch!"

Cool Papa Bell was reputed to be the fastest man in the game. Tiant would respond to that reputation by intentionally walking Bell on four pitches, just to set up their classic base-stealing duel.

"I knew he'd never get to second base," Tiant shrugs today.

Crowds flocked to watch Tiant pitch against Paige, or against Smokey Joe Williams, or Cannonball Jackman.

Tiant's team, the New York Cubans, played Yankee Stadium and the Polo Grounds, but always when the white inhabitants were on the road. All summer long he'd barnstorm with them, then return home each winter for the Cuban League season where thousands upon thousands of countrymen would come out to cheer for him.

Jim Higgins, a Boston University journalism professor who made several visits to Cuba in the early 1970s, discovered the extent of Tiant's popularity.

"Everywhere I went, people were familiar with the old man's name," he says. "It was like mentioning Ted Williams or Joe DiMaggio up here."

But the glory, the accouterments, and—most of all—the rewards that he and his fellow travelers in the colored leagues received were light-years removed from the trappings Williams, DiMaggio and their contemporaries were accustomed to.

"We made peanuts," the late Will Jackman reminisced a few years ago, shortly before his death in his drab three-story walkup situated in the heart of Boston's rundown South End. "If I was young today, I'm sure I'd be worth half a million. But I guess I've done everything in this life to make a dollar. I've worked in oil fields, driven trucks, dug ditches, cleaned people's houses. . . ."

Jackman painted a startling portrait of the way it was back then.

"I remember days when I played three games in the same uniform," he smiled. "If an arm or a leg hurt, you just wrapped something around it and kept on playing. There was no such thing as a whirlpool. We were lucky to get showers. And whenever we found a place with hot water, we were delighted. It didn't happen often. If we were treated the way players are treated today, we'd still be playing at 90."

There were, of course, no lavish pension funds for these men, no players' associations, no agents, no plans whatsoever for that inevitable day when time, their inexorable foe, would make them too old for what has always been a young man's game.

So in 1948, with a tired arm, a wife and an eight-year-old son to care for, Luis Eleuterio Tiant pooled his money with his brother-in-law and purchased a truck. At the age of 42, the man who may have been Cuba's greatest sports star ever began a second career as a furniture mover.

It's probably useless to ponder what might have been. Would barroom buffs be debating the comparative talents of Cy Young and Satchel Paige? Of Walter Johnson and Cannonball Jackman? Of Warren Spahn and Luis Tiant?

Tiant just shrugged at the question.

So did Will Jackman, 11 months before he died in a lonely tenement flat at the age of 75.

"I'm not bitter," the gray and weakened Cannonball said.

"That's just the way things were. There's no sense in thinking about what might have been."

The families of Nicanor del Campo were hardly affluent. If you were a professional worker, or if you owned land, life was pleasant enough in the Havana of the fifties. Otherwise, like most of the families in the Tiants' neighborhood, you worked hard to make ends meet.

Luis' father lugged furniture, and his mother cooked in other ladies' homes, and together they planned a better future for their son. Most of the kids in Luis' crowd attended public school, but his parents worked to send him to a private school.

"The public school only met in the mornings," he remembers. "But the private school met mornings and afternoons, so my mother made me go there in order to get more education. And my father made me learn English. He told me someday it might be important. I often think about that now."

But though he applied himself enough to achieve passing grades, Luis never fell in love with books or classrooms. His days really began the moment classes ended.

"My father owned a fruit market," Quintana says, "and I had to make deliveries for him, so I didn't always have a lot of time to play ball. But Luis never had to do much work as a kid. He was not rich, but his father and mother both worked and took real good care of him. Don't forget, he was an only child. There were four kids in my family. I can remember sitting on the ground playing marbles and seeing Luis come along from school. He'd be dressed all nice and neat, but he'd sit right down there with us anyway, getting his clothes dirty while he played. 'My mother would whip me if I did that,' I'd tell him. But he'd just smile and keep on playing. Nothing ever bothered him."

But one thing—*baseball*—fascinated him.

"I didn't see my father pitch very much," he recalls. "I was still young when he retired. But I can remember my Uncle Rene taking me to the games as a child and letting me sit in the dugout with all of the players. I used to think those were monkeys down there in those tunnels, and my father's friends would laugh when my uncle told that. Then they'd play with me. I think I always loved baseball."

It was not unusual, therefore, that Luis joined the local Little League when he reached the qualifying age. The elder Tiant never pushed his son toward the game; indeed, if anything, he seemed reluctant to encourage Luis, perhaps thinking he didn't want his son to end up in a furniture truck as well. Schooling, he believed, was the only guarantee of a better life.

And yet he couldn't hide his pride when friends would mention little Luis' prowess, nor could he resist the occasional temptation to step in with sound coaching advice.

"He could throw hard as a little boy," Señor Tiant remembers, "even though the ball weighed a lot for him. Sometimes I would watch him, and when he did something wrong I would walk over and say, 'No, do it this way.' Then I would show him the right way."

The Little Leaguers played Saturday nights and Sunday afternoons on a field behind the local refinery, and the advanced abilities that once made him the scourge of *el remachado* again made Luis a physical threat to the well-being of his friends. League officials, taking note of their substandard lighting system, banned Tiant from pitching in night games.

"They said I might kill somebody," he explained.

That's not all they were saying.

"You can tell people are talking about you," Luis says. "When I was 10 and 11, people kept telling me I had my father's abilities. That's not good to tell a kid. If he starts thinking he's a superstar, it will hurt him."

Deep inside, though, Luis loved to hear it, for the abundant praise simply served to reaffirm the validity of a persistent dream he'd begun embracing as a child.

"Someday I wanted to be a professional player," he remembers. "I think every Little Leaguer feels that way in the beginning. All I wanted to do was play baseball."

Following Little League, Tiant advanced to the Juvenile League, a unique Cuban program that has no comparable American counterpart. Teen-aged athletes would be chosen for their local teams, and all across the country, in all six provinces, neighborhoods competed against neighborhoods. Scouts, many of whom were former Cuban League stars, would then scour these hometown teams and select the finest players for positions on the province teams. Province would then compete against province in nationally followed games.

Collections were usually taken during the neighborhood games, with proceeds earmarked for support of the provincial touring teams.

Tiant not only starred for the Havana team, but also earned a berth on the Cuban Juvenile League All-Star Team which traveled to Mexico City in 1957 to compete in an international tournament involving teams from the United States, Puerto Rico, Panama, Santo Domingo, Colombia, Venezuela and host country Mexico.

He was three months shy of his seventeenth birthday.

"There were big crowds there," he recalls, "but they didn't bother me at all. I pitched two games: one was a win and the other was a no-decision."

Wintertime, meanwhile, meant the Cuban League, that historic four-team circuit that was the perennial off-season home for many American major leaguers as well as for native stars like Señor Tiant.

The teams were Havana, Marianao, Almendares and Cienfuegos.

From the combined Cuban League rosters, the finest young homegrown talent was picked to play for the Havana Sugar Kings come summertime. The Sugar Kings began as an experiment by the old Washington Senators franchise which sponsored them in the Triple-A International League (so called because it included, in addition to Havana, teams from Montreal and Toronto). Though they lasted only five years, disbanding in 1961 when Cuba and the United States severed relations, the Sugar Kings paid the Senators handsome dividends in pitchers Pedro Ramos and Camilio Pascual, both of whom became major league standouts.

Luis continued to star in the Juvenile League in the summer of 1958, but his efforts to catch on with one of the four Cuban League teams that winter proved fruitless. He simply wasn't ready yet.

"As a boy, people kept looking at Tiant and saying he inherited his father's talents," Juanito Quintana explains. "But baseball in

Cuba is serious. Being so-and-so's son means nothing if you are not good enough. In the Cuban League, Tiant had to make his own way."

As the 1959 season approached, Luis decided to try out for the Sugar Kings, who'd again be spending the summer in the American minor leagues. That brought tension to the normally placid Tiant household.

"I think my father still had bad feelings about his own career," Luis said. "The colored leagues never paid him much money, and the major leagues didn't want him because he was black. He went through so many bad things like that. I think he was afraid I would have bad luck, too. But I tried to tell him this was 1959 and things were different now. He didn't care. He still wanted me to go to school."

Ironically, it was Mrs. Tiant—a gentle woman who, according to her husband, "doesn't know a thing about baseball"—who settled the issue.

"If this is what he wants to do," she counseled her husband, "then let him do it. This may be his only chance."

Señor Tiant looked at his wife, then at his son, then nodded his head in resignation.

When the Sugar Kings held tryouts that spring in Cerro Stadium, *el padre* Tiant accompanied his 18-year-old son. Luis didn't make the team. More than that, he was crushed by the manner in which he was rejected.

"Señor Tiant," a Washington official confided to the father at the end of the first day's practice, "your boy will never make it. He should accept that now, and maybe get a job in the fruit market as a salesman."

But as that door slammed shut, another one swung open.

Bobby Avila, the great Cleveland second baseman of the fifties, was now an Indians scout, searching Cuba for talent. He was also an old friend of the Tiant family, dating back to the days when he was the batboy for Señor Tiant's teams. Bobby knew of Luis' talents; indeed, he had followed his career since Luis was a Little Leaguer. And so he recommended him to Carlos Gonzalez, general manager of the Mexico City Tigers in the Mexican League, and Gonzalez responded with an offer: $150 a month.

Luis grabbed it. He didn't know where it would lead him, but at least it was a start. With his mother's love and his father's apprehension behind him, Tiant took off for Mexico City with a professional contract in his pocket.

That much of his dream had come true.

CHAPTER 2

A Tiger Meets Maria

Tiant's first season with the Tigers was equivalent to *The Perils of Pauline*. There were flashes of greatness in that overpowering fastball, in that unconventional and seemingly uncontrolled motion, so reminiscent of his famous father's delivery. And yet there were also periods of wild inefficiency when, indeed, the man who suggested a career in the fruit market appeared to have been a sage.

Young Tiant started 27 games and finished only 11 of them. He walked 107 and fanned only 98. He allowed a league-leading 139 runs, accounting for his monstrous 5.92 ERA. The result, predictably, was 19 losses in 24 decisions.

And yet three of those five victories were complete game shutouts, one of which was a thing of beauty in which he struck out Frank Howard, the Dodgers' prized minor league prodigy, three times! Los Angeles officials were so taken aback by that performance that they immediately attempted to purchase Tiant's contract from the Mexico City club, but Gonzalez cooled their enthusiasm by demanding $40,000. They had been impressed, but not *that* impressed. So Tiant remained a Tiger.

Returning home that fall, Luis felt quite sure the Cuban League would, at last, recognize its terrible oversight of a year ago and welcome him to its bosom. After all, he was no longer just the son of Luis Eleuterio Tjant; he was now a Mexico City Tiger—a professional ballplayer, if you please—and more than likely there'd be a mad rush to secure his services.

Instead, there was massive indifference.

It soon became apparent that he was not going to be wooed by any of the Cuban League members, so the only remaining course was to join the rest of the job-seekers at tryout camp.

Luis had known Monchy de Arcos, part owner of the Almendares team, for some time now. In fact, de Arcos let him work out with the squad during Tiant's days in the Juvenile League. So Luis figured Almendares was his surest bet to make the league. Every day, for almost a month, he boarded a bus in Nicanor del Campo and made the 45-minute trip to the tryout camp at Ciudad de Los Portes. All during that time he received no remuneration, not even for food or travel expenses. Nobody gave him any indication he would survive the pending roster cuts.

Exasperated, he finally stalked into de Arcos' office.

"I've been coming here for a month at my own expense," he said, "and I can't afford to keep doing that. So tell me now. I want to know if you're going to give me an opportunity."

De Arcos nodded sympathetically, then explained he did not intend to award any contracts to pitchers.

Luis was on the next bus home, and the following day he showed up at Havana's tryout camp. Manager Fermin Guerra, about to break camp, found a spot on his roster for Tiant, but when the team kicked off its season with a prolonged losing streak, Guerra released Luis and promised to call him when things got better.

"He never called again," Tiant remembers.

So Luis packed his bags and took off for winter ball in Nicaragua, once again frustrated in his efforts to play in Cuba's most prestigious league.

As he headed back to Mexico City in the spring of 1960, Luis had no way of knowing that the coming months would be major turning points in both his personal and professional lives.

The Mexico City Tigers immediately began to reap the rewards of their long-suffering 1959 season. They had been young and in-experienced and incohesive that summer, and they paid the stand-ard price as the rest of the Mexican League knocked them around rather regularly. But now they returned with more polished skills, and no one better exemplified that new look than Tiant, whose winter in Nicaragua had provided him with much-needed playing time. The fastball had more velocity than ever, but, more impor-tant, the erraticism that had caused Carlos Gonzalez to ride an emotional roller coaster whenever Luis pitched the preceding sum-mer now appeared to be more subdued.

That's not to say his 19-year-old *wunderkind* was now a finished product, however. On the contrary, Luis led the league in walks (124) and still had an oversized ERA (4.65), but the promise of future stardom seemed to shine brighter as the season rolled along. Tiant's final 17–7 record tied him for the league lead in victories, and he was a central figure in the playoffs as the Ti-gers went on to win the Mexican League championship.

Throughout that 1960 season Mexico City was slightly agog over the Tigers, and members of the team were generally treated as celebrities wherever they went. Their pictures were spread across the daily papers and in the pages of weekly magazines like *El Figaro* and *Deporte Ilustrado*. Tiant was particularly in demand at clinics throughout the city, where he'd spend hours counseling youngsters and discussing the finer points of *juego de pelota,* the game of baseball.

But the night of July 28, a warm Thursday evening, belonged to Luis. There was no game and no commitments on his schedule, so it sounded like a good idea when his teammate and pal Luis Zayas suggested they drop by a local softball diamond where a couple of girls teams had a contest set for after supper. Luis watched the game impassively, enjoying Zayas' good-natured commentaries, until his attention was sharply diverted when the home team came off the field at the close of the fourth inning.

¡¡Caramba!! He couldn't take his eyes off the left fielder as she made her way back to the bench.

"She was lookin' good," he smiles, remembering that first im-pression.

Indeed, Señorita Maria del Refugio Navarro was a stunning

lady whose talents went far beyond her softball skills. She loved folk dancing and music and ballet as well, and often performed those arts in local shows and reviews. The Social Security office where she worked sponsored many of these outside activities, including the softball team—which brings us back to Luis.

"I remember seeing him sitting there as I came off the field," she says. "He was blowing kisses at me, and I kept wondering, 'What's the matter with him?'"

Then she dismissed him from her mind, but the following night their paths crossed again when one of her teammates hosted a party that Zayas accepted an invitation to, bringing Tiant in tow.

Although most of the girls knew Zayas, and were at least familiar with the fact that Luis was the star pitcher for the Tigers, Maria had no idea who he was.

Tiant's ego was not damaged. In fact, her unawareness of his status made her even more appealing to him.

"Almost all of my life I've been known as Tiant the ballplayer," he explains. "If people recognize me, okay. It is the way I make my living. But I've never gone around telling people who I am. I don't believe in that. I think you should just be yourself, and be accepted for that. I've always wanted people to like me because I'm me, not because I'm a ballplayer."

Maria didn't particularly like him for either reason when the party began.

But there was one thing that caught her attention.

"His stockings," she smiled. "I never liked those low socks most men wore. Luis was wearing nice high stockings that night. That's the first thing I noticed about him."

While Luis was blowing kisses and laying on the charm, his stockings were actually scoring all of the points.

When the music began he asked her to dance, and they stayed out there most of the evening, getting acquainted while the party went on without them. When the last dance was played they were still together, and both of them knew it wouldn't be their last dance at all.

"When I first saw him at the party, I think I was afraid," she remembers. "He kept staring at me with those big eyes. But then we began dancing—and that was it!"

Just like that?

She smiled again and nodded. "Just like that."

As the party broke up and moved outside, Maria returned to the girls she had come with and prepared to step inside a taxi.

Then she felt a tapping on her shoulder and turned to face Luis.

"Hey," he suggested, "give me a kiss."

"No," she replied, pretending to scold him with her eyes.

The taxi's door closed, and Tiant stood at the curb watching its tail lights disappear around a corner.

But they would meet again many times that summer, never really saying goodbye until Luis finally left for Cuba the first week in October.

Luis was still thinking about Maria and the Mexican League championship and all of the good times the summer had brought him when his plane touched down at José Marti International Airport in Havana. Named after one of Cuba's greatest writers, the airport was a bustling center of activity until the age of the jumbo jets reduced it to an outpost. Now it was a tranquil site.

But on this particular afternoon, as the plane taxied in from the runway, Luis could see a welcoming committee awaiting his arrival. It included his parents and the man who had never returned the promised call—Fermin Guerra, manager of the Havana team in the Cuban League.

As soon as the obligatory greetings were exchanged, Guerra began his sales pitch, telling Luis how much he looked forward to having him on the club in the season that was just around the corner.

Señor Tiant—perhaps remembering those glorious years when he pitched for Havana—looked on approvingly as Guerra completed his delivery to the son now about to follow in those famous footsteps.

But Luis, still remembering the hurt and disappointment of the preceding year when Monchy de Arcos rejected him from Almendares and Guerra cut him loose from Havana, was plainly unimpressed.

"I don't want to sign with him," Luis told his startled father, who had shared Guerra's enthusiasm. "He didn't give me the opportunity last year. He lied to me. He threw me away. Now we win a championship and he wants to have me. Why should I come back to him?"

Guerra's protestations fell upon deaf ears as Luis gathered his parents and luggage and headed for the family homestead and the quiet surroundings of Nicanor del Campo.

But Guerra persisted, continuing to visit Tiant's home, and Luis was eventually persuaded to forgive, if not forget.

And chances are, in his heart of hearts, he never regretted that decision. The cheering crowds at Tropical Park and Cerro Stadium—the same *aficionados* who had once roared their approval of *el padre's* pitching genius—now threw their unequivocal support behind his handsome namesake.

Those were memories that Luis would savor for a lifetime, and it was fortunate that he took advantage of them in 1960, for he would never have a chance to play in the Cuban League again.

From the earliest stages of Luis' career, dating back to his days as a Little Leaguer, observers predicted his unorthodox motion would cause his arm to burn out prematurely.

"I remember the time I went with the Juvenile League team to the world tournament in Mexico City," he says. "There were a lot of scouts at those games, and many of them said I would never make it to the big leagues. They said I threw sidearm too much and I was going to hurt myself."

To this day, Tiant steadfastly maintains that his style is comfortable for him, that it places no undue stress on his body. And yet he's had a history of temporary injuries, beginning in the summer of 1961 when he returned to Mexico City for what would be his third and final season with the Tigers.

He appeared in only 24 games that year, down from 41 in both of his first two seasons, but he still managed to post a 12–9 record with 141 strikeouts.

The highlight of that baseball season came at the annual Pan American Association All-Star Game, pitting the finest stars from the Mexican League against their counterparts in the Texas League. The Texas roster was abundant with future major leaguers like Joe Pepitone, Jim Bouton, Phil Linz and Tommy Aaron.

Luis didn't start that day. That honor, ironically, went to Julio

(Jiqui) Moreno, a well-traveled veteran who had once been a teammate of Señor Tiant's. But Luis was credited with the victory after striking out six during his three-inning stint.

Up in the grandstand, meanwhile, one particular observer was taking special notice of every Tiant pitch. Monchy de Arcos, the part owner of the Almendares team, was there in his other capacity as a scout for the Cleveland Indians.

Monchy liked what he saw and filed an appropriate report.

When the season ended, the Indians purchased Luis' contract from Carlos Gonzales for $35,000.

And his star continued to rise.

Beginning with the Thursday afternoon in May when he flew in from Cuba, Luis had divided his 1961 summer schedule between the Tigers and Maria. When he wasn't at the ball park, he was usually with her. Friends became accustomed to seeing them together, and no doubt most of them fully expected to hear wedding bells before long.

Monday, June 12, was an off-day for the Tigers, a chance to catch their breath and attend to personal matters. And Luis had a very personal matter to attend to that evening, one that had his stomach in knots by sundown.

The so-called age of sophistication had done away with a lot of the niceties and traditions that enriched the years gone by, but in Mexico City, in 1961, a young man thinking of making a young lady his wife was still expected to visit her family and formally ask for her hand.

As the appointed hour drew nigh, Luis' nerves were hopping like his changeup. He stalked his apartment, rubbing his moist palms and repeating—for maybe the seventy-fifth time—the words he would use that night.

"I would like . . ."

"Would you do me the honor . . ."

"Maria and I have been talking . . ."

He paced some more, then in despair he called his pal Luis Zayas. It had been Zayas who brought them together in the first place. And it had been Zayas who helped Luis win a crucial 1960 playoff game by stealing home. Zayas was the kind of friend who was always there when you needed him.

And, at this moment, Tiant decided he needed him very much.

When Maria opened the door of her home that night, there was her future husband, forcing a shaky smile at her.

And there was Luis Zayas, standing right beside him!

"I was afraid to go alone," he laughs, looking back across the years. "I made Zayas come inside the house with me when I asked."

Because Maria's father was deceased, permission had to be granted by her mother and by her two older brothers, Rafael and Hipolito.

When the hellos and how-are-yous had been exhausted and everyone had been seated, a silence fell upon the room.

Luis licked his lips, cleared his throat and directed his eyes from Maria and Zayas over to his hosts, Señora Navarro and Señores Navarro.

And then he blurted: *"I want the hand!"*

The brothers nodded, the mother smiled, and one washed-out Mexico City Tiger released a weary sigh of relief.

Tiant and Zayas remained for another 90 minutes, laughing and drinking with Rafael and Hipolito.

But what if the brothers had said no?

"Then I'd have told them, 'I'm going to marry him anyway!' " Maria shrugs. "And they would have said, 'No, no, no; you have permission.' "

On August 12, Luis and Maria were married. With permission.

CHAPTER 3

Castro's Cuba

Throughout 1959, 1960 and 1961, years in which Tiant's life centered around Mexico City, his homeland was in the throes of a tumultuous transition from the government of Fulgencio Batista to the government of Fidel Castro. It was more than just an exchange of power. It was a violent revolution, and its victims numbered more than just the soldiers and the politicians. It would eventually affect the lives of every Cuban, for it unalterably changed the very life of this idyllic, beautiful island, where the year-round temperature averages 77 degrees, where more than 3,000 varieties of fruits and flowers abound, and where spotless sandy shorelines are daily washed by waters of the Atlantic, Caribbean and Gulf of Mexico.

The Pearl of the Antilles it was called, and indeed it is.

Batista's power began in 1933 when he led the successful conspiracy that resulted in the ouster of the tyrannical Machado regime. A succession of administrations appeared in the ensuing years, but Batista—as chief of staff of the Cuban Constitutional Army—remained virtually the most powerful man in the country. That power was formalized in 1940 when he ran for President and was elected. Following World War II, in accordance with

Cuba's Constitution, Batista called for a new election, even though the law of the land prohibited him from succeeding himself in office.

He surfaced again as a presidential candidate in 1952, but three months before the scheduled June elections—with the support of the Cuban Army—he decided to forcefully overthrow the government of incumbent President Carlos Prio Socarras, later explaining to the people that he feared Socarras had planned to sabotage the results.

As he assumed office for the second time in 12 years, Batista announced that he would remain President only long enough to restore normalcy to Cuban life and to arrange for fair and honest elections as soon as possible. Seven months later he conducted a campaign and was elected without opposition.

In the years that followed, Batista's regime was rife with corruption. Disenchantment grew across the countryside as student groups, labor forces and professional ranks expressed their anger. Civil warfare flared in 1956 when a small group of anti-Batista activists—led by a young attorney named Fidel Castro—staged an attack on government forces. Less than a year later a band of students unsuccessfully tried to storm the Presidential Palace and assassinate Batista. The Catholic Church, representing a vast majority of the Cuban population, implored Batista to step aside in the interests of restoring peace.

His answer to all of this was a reign of terror in which as many as 20,000 dissidents were killed by Batista forces between 1956 and New Year's Day, 1959—none of whom enjoyed the benefit of legal process before their deaths.

In the early morning hours of January 1, 1959, shortly after a 3,000-man garrison of Batista troops had been routed by 300 rebels in the Battle of Santa Clara, Batista gathered his closest aides and fled the country.

It had been a political revolution, more than an economic revolution, and the triumphant Castro—at the age of 32—told his followers what they wanted to hear. There would be new elections, he promised, and a return to democracy. And so they lined the streets of Havana on January 8 to cheer his arrival in the capital city.

Within a month of his ascension to power, however, many of

his idealistic supporters began to have doubts about the regime they had just swept into office. A wave of military trials began, followed by the execution of remaining Batista aides. Toward the end of 1959 the Castro government began expropriating property owned by investors from the United States.

Then, early in 1960, Castro hosted Anastas Mikoyan, one of the highest-ranking Soviet officials, and together they ironed out economic agreements that would bind their nations. In effect, Cuba would exchange sugar for machinery, but the pact also carried overtones of a military alignment as well. By the end of 1960, Castro proclaimed what had already been obvious for a long time: Cuba was a socialist state, modeled after the Soviet Union.

Within a year, diplomatic relations with the United States would be severed, and an embargo would be placed on all Cuban goods destined for American ports.

Real estate holdings and savings accounts were confiscated by the new government as the vestiges of democracy grew practically extinct.

It was probably not surprising that in the first two years of Castro's regime more than 500,000 Cubans—nearly 10 per cent of the population—left their homeland for good.

It was clearly a rebuke and it would not do. Besides the obvious political ramifications of such a mass exodus, Castro faced a practical problem as well. Who would harvest the crops if all the workers fled? Who would dispense the medicine and teach the students and staff the institutions if all the professionals decided to emigrate? Indeed, who would be left?

So, in 1961, measures were taken to drastically curtail departures from the island. Men between 15 and 35 were automatically excluded because they were of military age. Others intending to leave had to apply to the government for permission. If the permission was granted, it was contingent on several conditions. A three-year waiting period was established, during which time the individual would be considered an enemy of the state. That meant loss of his job and forfeiture of all personal belongings. The three years would be spent in government service, which usually translated into menial agricultural labor.

After all that, emigration still would not be seen as automatic.

In short, free egress was all but eliminated as hard times fell upon the Pearl of the Antilles.

In early summer of 1961, Juanito Quintana knew the time was short. If he didn't move quickly, he'd probably spend the rest of his life in a Cuba whose future had suddenly grown misty.

Estela, his fiancée, had a sister in Chicago. She had lived there for 10 years and had become a naturalized American citizen.

So the sister claimed Estela, who then flew north to join her.

As soon as she was settled, Estela married Juanito by proxy.

Then she claimed him, and he flew north as well.

In rapid-fire actions, Quintana managed to get his parents, his brothers, his sister, his nephews, his uncles and his cousins out of Cuba before the doors were slammed shut.

"I didn't want to leave," he says today. "But I came for the same reason most of the others left. The government. And I've never been back home since."

In July of 1961, Jorge Raspall—little Jorgito—also managed to get out, just one month after his future wife, Olga, had departed.

"I thought I would never see him again," she remembers.

With two young daughters and a good career, Raspall's roots have now reached deep into American soil.

"It would be hard for any of us to go back again," he says. "It would be hard on the children especially, because they were born and brought up here. But I still think of Cuba often. It was the most beautiful country you'd ever want to see."

Abelardo Aguiar—the little friend who lost the bananas the day he played *el remachado* with Luis—wasn't as lucky as the others.

He died before a Castro firing squad.

Then there was Felix Fernandez.

Felix, who would become one of Luis' dearest friends in the States, first met him in 1958 when Luis was finishing high school and Felix was pitching for the University of Havana, where he earned his doctorate in philosophy and law.

When Luis moved on to professional ball in 1959, their paths temporarily separated.

Felix had been one of the bright young minds supporting Castro's cause, and his brother Julio had been one of Fidel's top lieutenants in the early stages of the revolution.

"But when Castro became a Communist we knew we could not live under that system," Felix explains. "It was against our principles. We were sure the people of Cuba would have no freedom after that."

Julio was the first to leave, hijacking a Cuban patrol boat and forcing its crew to take him to Florida.

That left Felix in a precarious position, for the DGI—the Castro intelligence organization patterned after Russia's KGB— looked upon him with suspicion.

"They felt I might be planning underground activities against him," Fernandez says.

But what he was planning, instead, was an escape. And he managed it, leaving under the cover of night, under an assumed name, in April of 1962.

"All I had with me were the clothes on my back," he recalls. "Cuba left a lot to be desired under Batista, but we had about 16 papers in those days, and all of them were criticizing him. No one criticized Castro. There was no such thing as democracy. And so I left."

Since their marriage took place in the middle of the 1961 season, Luis and Maria decided they'd postpone their honeymoon until the fall. Then, accompanied by Luis Zayas and his wife, they'd stop off at Nicanor del Campo, where Maria would get to meet her in-laws for the first time. When that visit concluded, the foursome would head for Island de Pinos, a beautiful hideaway— perfect for a honeymoon—just off the southern coast of Cuba, surrounded by the crystal-clear Caribbean.

Toward the end of the second week in September 1961, as Maria began packing their suitcases, Luis went over to the telephone and placed a call to his father, just to let him know when to expect them.

He simply wasn't prepared for what followed.

"Luis," Señor Tiant said softly, "stay in Mexico. Don't come home. There's nothing for you here now. Stay where you are and make a good life for your family."

Luis just didn't understand. He had been apolitical all his life, just as his father had been. What did politics have to do with baseball? What did politics have to do with him?

Señor Tiant wasn't sure he knew the answers, either. But he knew that the better life he and his wife had always desired for their child, the one they had scrimped and saved for, was no longer to be found in Cuba. At least not now. *Mañana* perhaps. But at the moment the decision was irreversible.

"I'll let you know when you can come," he promised.

Luis was torn asunder.

"That's why you have to love your parents," he says today. "No matter how much it hurts them, all they want is what's best for you. That's their only consideration. From the time you're a baby, they always watch out for you. You'll never find two other people like them in the world."

So the honeymoon plans were abandoned, and so were the plans to pitch in the Cuban League (which Castro disbanded anyway).

Instead, Luis and Maria headed to Puerto Rico where he would spend the winter preparing for whatever the Cleveland Indians had in mind for him come the spring of 1962.

Fifteen years would pass before Luis saw his father again. In that time Señor Tiant would grow old and gray; Luis and Maria would have three handsome children; and the 90 miles which separate Cuba from American soil would continue to separate loved ones.

Reggie Smith, once a teammate in Boston, observed: "Luis wakes up every morning with something funny to say."

Indeed, Tiant became one of the most delightful characters in baseball, a constant source of locker room entertainment, a truly funny guy.

Tommy Harper, who'd play with him in Cleveland and Boston and become his closest friend in baseball—not to mention the butt of his very best pranks—knew Luis well enough to occasionally peek behind the happy façade and see the sober man inside.

"Sometimes I could just feel there was something underneath," Tommy explains. "I knew he was happy with his career, and I knew he really enjoyed his friends, but it was always on his mind that his parents weren't able to share in his success."

Luis didn't talk about it often, except with friends like Diego Segui and other Latin ballplayers who were caught up in the same web of personal tragedy.

But there's little doubt this constant sorrow contributed to another Tiant trait. Luis rarely lost his temper, or got exercised when someone pulled a boner that cost him a ball game. His philosophy seemed to be a simple matter of *Que sera, sera*. Managers and teammates marveled at the man's composure under fire. And even when he was down and out—as we shall see—Tiant remained unruffled.

Years later, in an unguarded moment, he reflected just a bit.

"We think we have so many problems as we go through life, but then some *real* problems come along and we start to realize that all of the other ones just weren't that important. Family problems can hurt so much. Like seeing your son ill and not being able to do anything about it. Or watching your father die and not being able to stop it. I see my fellow Cubans in this country and I watch them suffer because of the things that are happening back home, and I suffer with them. I know of some whose parents have died and they couldn't even go home to bury them. That's not right. Those problems hurt so badly. Sometimes I think about my father dying. I try not to, but I can't help it. When you talk about problems like that, no other problems can seem big or important."

PART II
A Career Takes Shape

CHAPTER 4

The Minor Leaguer

So now Luis was a professional baseball player in America, the land that claims the game as its own, the same land, ironically, which once diluted that game by prohibiting stars like Señor Tiant from engaging in major league competition.

Now the opportunity that eluded the father was knocking for the son.

Perhaps Luis' assignment to Charleston, South Carolina, the Indians' Class A affiliate in the Eastern League, would have been nothing to write home about for anybody else, but in his mind it was nothing less than a visit to Wonderland.

At least it seemed that way for a while.

"When I was younger I used to look at Minnie Minoso and dream of being just like he was. It seemed like a long way off, and maybe it would never happen, I told myself. Who knows about those things as a child? But now here I was, coming to America to play, and it seemed like my dreams were coming true."

Luis won his first five games, then his elbow stiffened. When he finally returned to the lineup his pitches had nothing on them. He was throwing in pain, and the hitters were having a field day. Time, he kept telling himself, was the only answer.

Then manager Johnny Lipon called him into his office one day and told Luis that Cleveland had decided to promote him to its Jacksonville club in the Triple-A International League.

"You know I've got a bad arm, Johnny," he protested. "It makes no sense to go upstairs."

"But that's what they want," Lipon replied.

"Why not send one of the kids who have good arms?" Luis persisted.

"Because they want *you!*" Lipon explained.

Tiant was plainly frustrated.

"It's not that I don't want to go up there," he said. "I just want to go when I feel good. I don't want to go when I'm hurt. I can't do anything up there now."

Lipon shrugged helplessly. Tiant had a point, he knew, but major league franchises do not have a history of consulting Class A players for points they might like to raise.

The following day Luis arrived in Columbus, Ohio, where Jacksonville had a game. He was put in for one inning, during which he walked two batters, and then he was never used again.

"I just ran and ran every day, trying to stay in shape," he remembers. "But they wouldn't use me. It was like belonging to a track club instead of a baseball team."

A month later Jacksonville formally rejected him, shipping him back to Johnny Lipon in Charleston.

The long layoff, coming on the heels of his injury, rendered Luis practically useless for the remainder of the summer. His final record was 7–8.

Winter, and its baseball season in Mexico, couldn't come fast enough.

But Luis had a much better reason for wanting to get home to the apartment in Mexico City. Maria had remained there throughout the summer, pregnant with their first child. And now the baby was waiting for his father's arrival.

On the morning on September 5, well into the homestretch of the schedule, Luis had arrived at the Charleston ball park to board the bus that would haul the squad north to Elmira. When he got there a telegram was waiting, informing him that Maria had just given birth to a boy.

His name, like his father's and grandfather's, would be Luis.

The news thrilled Luis, and all the way to Elmira his thoughts were of his newborn son.

"After everything that had happened back in Cuba, this meant so much," he recalled. "If I had been alone, on my own, I might have gone into a hole. But now I had responsibilities: a wife, a baby, a home. I had to take care of them. And that made me feel happy."

Maria's anxiety matched her husband's as the reunion drew near.

"When the baby came I wanted Luis to be with me," she remembers. "All of the other ladies had their husbands beside them and I didn't have mine. I missed him so much."

It was a happy winter for the three of them. Luis was finally pitching well again, and the baby brought a new dimension of love into their lives.

The only sad moments came during the holidays.

How could he make "Merry Christmas!" sound cheerful over the phone?

He didn't even try to. He would just tell his mother and father how beautiful little Luis was, how fast he was growing, how things were going in winter ball . . . and how very much he loved them.

Then he would hand the receiver to Maria, the daughter-in-law they had never met, and she would proceed to fill in the holes of his report.

And, invariably, the goodbyes would leave them shaken.

"We were always a close family when I was growing up," Tiant remembers. "And the holidays were always special. Relatives and friends would come to our house, and they'd eat and drink and laugh. Those were very happy times for me and for my parents. After I left Cuba, there was always a sadness to the holidays. I couldn't see my parents. I couldn't even send them anything. And talking on the phone was never easy. You couldn't really say the things that were on your mind."

What Luis really wanted to say—what always surfaced whenever he allowed himself to reminisce—was basically "Thank you," because, like most children grown up, he'd come to realize and appreciate the meaning of parental love.

"We were kind of poor when I was a kid," he says, "but thank God I never went hungry. My mother and father took good care of me. Maybe I never went to Harvard University or anything like that, but I had a good home, and my parents taught me the important things, like respect for authority and how to conduct myself before people. They loved me a lot."

In the spring of 1963 Luis was invited to the Cleveland Indians training camp. The fact that he was cut—which, of course, came as no surprise—didn't diminish the thrill of having at least visited the Promised Land of the major leagues. He was still just 23 years old. His day would come, he was sure. Meanwhile, he would improve.

Instead of returning him to Charleston, the Tribe decided to assign Luis to its Burlington, North Carolina, club in the Class A Carolina League where he enjoyed—in his words—"one hell of a year."

Indeed, in addition to posting a fine 14–9 record, and completing 17 of his 24 starts, Luis led the league in strikeouts (207) while bringing his ERA down to 2.56, his best mark since he began playing professional ball with the Mexico City Tigers in 1959. The highlight of that season was a splendid no-hit effort against Winston-Salem, the Boston representative in the league.

When he returned home to Maria and Luis that fall, en route to winter ball in Venezuela, he was sure he'd be wearing a Cleveland uniform when another springtime rolled around.

The 1963 Indians, under new manager Birdie Tebbetts, had tied with Detroit for fifth place in the American League. They were just two victories shy of the .500 mark, but 25½ games off the pace of Ralph Houk's pennant-winning Yankees, who finished with 104 triumphs. Their winningest pitchers were Jack Kralick and Jim Grant with 13 victories apiece, but Grant ended up as an overall loser with 14 defeats.

So the spring of 1964 seemed like an ideal time for a fresh young arm to appear at the Cleveland training camp.

And three of them did.

Sam McDowell had been in the Indians' system since 1961, and now the word had it that he was finally ready for full-time service with the big team.

Sonny Siebert, even though he had a disappointing (4–10) season in Jacksonville in 1963, had been highly touted by every Cleveland scout.

And then there was Tiant—or rather, then there almost wasn't Tiant. In what appears to have been an incredible oversight, the Indians failed to place Luis on their list of protected players following his superb season in Burlington. Even though they were aware of his potential, they were pretty sure the rest of the baseball world didn't know the guy from Adam. Then Luis went to Venezuela during the winter and, in one stretch, hurled six consecutive shutouts.

Now the Cleveland office was in a tizzy.

"We knew we had made a mistake, but it was too late to rectify it," says Yankees president Gabe Paul, who was then the Cleveland general manager. "So we sweated out the draft, and when Luis wasn't taken it was one of the greatest reliefs I've ever had."

When the Tribe broke camp in early April, Siebert headed to Cleveland with the parent squad. McDowell was dispatched to Portland, the AAA farm team in the Pacific Coast League. And Tiant—much to his great chagrin, especially in view of the fact that he had pitched well in the exhibition games—was ordered back to Burlington.

"It was one of the best springs I ever had," he remembers. "I really thought I had a chance to stay."

He did get a surprise promotion, however, the day before he was due to leave for North Carolina. Johnny Lipon, his old manager back in Charleston, was now managing the Portland club and he had just received word that one of his hurlers had sustained an injury. So he sought and received permission to bring Luis to Portland with him.

It wasn't the major leagues, and it wasn't as if the Indians had really believed he belonged there, but Tiant gladly swapped his tickets and then hopped the plane to Oregon.

Opportunity was knocking, and that was good enough.

But the moment he walked into the Beavers' clubhouse and

drew a uniform, he understood he wasn't exactly the kid they'd all been waiting for.

"You should have seen the uniform they gave me!" he says. "It had patches and holes all over it. And it was so big you could have put two of me into it."

Almost as if to save the rest of the squad from this walking eyesore, Luis was assigned to a locker that he suspected was on the other side of the county line. Except for Hector Cardenas, who had been sentenced to the adjacent locker, Tiant had no neighbors whatsoever.

"It was like they were hiding us," he remembers, shaking his head. "We were way over in this corner, so squeezed in we could hardly get out. I looked at Hector and said, 'I can't believe they'd do this to players.' He couldn't believe it either."

As a result, Luis wasn't too surprised when opening day arrived and he wasn't included in Portland's starting rotation. Judging by what had transpired so far, he was probably relieved that no one had asked him to pay his way into the ball park.

He'd show them all, he believed, but he'd have to bide his time just a bit longer.

His chance finally came when McDowell was unable to finish a game. Lipon beckoned Luis from the end of the bench and sent him out to relieve Sam.

Tiant worked four brilliant innings, striking out eight, and—as he recalls—"from that day on I had a job."

And what a job he did!

He won his first eight games in a row, lost a 2–0 heartbreaker, then reeled off another seven victories in succession for a fabulous record of 15–1. His fastball stood the league on its ear, and when he wasn't "bringing in the heat" he was positively baffling batters with a veritable kaleidoscope of unnamed pitches—though opponents certainly had names for them!—that seemed to come from all directions and at any speed he felt like choosing. In the 137 innings he worked, Luis recorded 154 strikeouts while issuing only 40 walks.

He was *el jefe* on the mound. The boss.

CHAPTER 5

A Dramatic Debut

Russ Schneider was halfway through the first year of what would become a prolific career as Cleveland's top baseball writer, and like any other smart reporter he had already learned two of the most basic tenets of the trade: (a) do your own homework, and (b) cultivate your own sources of information. Gabe Paul was such a source.

That's why, early on a Friday morning, July 17, 1964, Schneider found himself sweating in a steam bath for the first time in his life.

"Gabe is just nuts about them," he explained. "Every town he goes to, he tries to find a steam bath."

In New York, of course, where the Cleveland entourage had just arrived for the start of a weekend series in Yankee Stadium, you can find just about anything you're looking for—steam baths included.

"But he didn't want to go alone," Russ remembers, "so he talked me into going with him."

After they had been sitting in the torrid cabinets for a while, Paul turned toward the gasping writer and said, "Oh, by the way, we're going to bring up Tiant today."

Schneider suddenly felt trapped.

"It was a story," he says, "but there wasn't a damned thing I could do about it sitting in that place."

But at least he wouldn't have to call the office for background material to use in his piece.

"That whole winter leading up to the 1964 season I knew I was going to get the baseball job," Schneider recalls, "so I really prepared myself by digging through all the books I could find on kids who were coming up through the system. And I knew we had two super pitchers at Portland in McDowell and Tiant. Sam had been up and down a few times, so people around Cleveland knew who he was, but there really had been no exposure at all on Tiant. I remembered, though, that Hoot Evers, who worked in the farm system, once told me: 'Watch this guy. He had some arm trouble, but if he can avoid any more he's going to be something.'"

And he had been something in Portland, all right.

So Birdie Tebbetts asked Paul to deliver him.

While the Indians were pulling into New York that Friday morning, the Portland Beavers were flying into San Diego, arriving at 8 A.M. to find that little seaport city all agog over the upcoming duel between Tiant—the scourge of the Pacific Coast League—and hard-hitting Tony Perez, the star of the hometown Padres.

Banner headlines in the local papers ballyhooed their celebrated showdown, complete with Tony's picture, and the Beavers found themselves caught up in the fervor, too, by the time they arrived at their hotel.

As soon as Luis entered his room, intent on reading more about what Perez planned to do to his fastball, his phone began ringing. It was manager Johnny Lipon, asking him to please come over to his room.

Tiant put down the paper and went to see what Lipon wanted.

"I just got a call from Gabe," Johnny smiled. "They want you, Luis. Right away. So don't unpack your bags. Congratulations."

It was the kind of news Johnny liked to deliver, even if it did mean he was losing his finest pitcher, because guys who work in the minors see so many kids who fritter away their talents, or maybe never get the right break, or perhaps don't take advantage of the break when it's offered. The minor leagues are just a land of hopes and dreams, but now and then a special kid will come along, and men like Lipon know it will only be a matter of time before he'll have the whole world cheering.

When you're surrounded by so many disappointments, so many failures and so many rude awakenings, you find yourself sharing in the enjoyment when really good news comes. You might even allow yourself the satisfaction of thinking perhaps you had a hand in it.

And this was wonderful news for Luis.

Or so Johnny thought.

You can imagine his sense of incredulity, therefore to find that Luis was disgusted with the idea.

Although he had kept his feelings to himself, he had spent most of the season seething over what he believed—or imagined—were subtle affronts from the organization. The spring training decision to return him to Burlington really got under his skin, even though it was rescinded. They'd have sent him there if someone on the Portland roster hadn't been injured, and that was tantamount to telling him that he clearly hadn't impressed them yet.

The tattered uniform and remote locker he was issued upon his arrival in Portland didn't do anything to improve his frame of mind.

But the final indignity, the one that really rankled him, had come a month earlier, when he and McDowell had identical 8–0 records. The Indians called for Sam and never mentioned Luis.

"Why did they wait until I had 15 wins before they decided they liked me?" he demanded of Lipon. "Now more than half of the year is gone and they tell me to come. Well, I don't want to go."

"Don't fool yourself, Luis," Johnny implored. "This is your big opportunity."

"They didn't treat me right," Tiant fumed.

By now Lipon was completely perplexed. He could understand his pitcher's reasons for feeling hurt, and yet he knew Luis could not be allowed to gamble his future on a moment of pique.

"Luis," he said softly, "I know how you feel, and I don't blame you. You're too good to be here. But now you have a chance to show everybody that you belong up there. We both know you can do the job. But it's up to you to prove it to everyone else. Don't throw this opportunity away. It's too important. You've got to go."

Lipon, of course, was absolutely right, and Luis knew it. Everything he had done in baseball, from Little League to Juvenile League to Cuban League to Mexican League to Eastern League to Carolina League and now to International League, not to mention his father's dreams and now his own responsibilities for Maria and little Luis—everything had been predicated on this very moment when the American major leagues—"the great leagues," as Juanito Quintana called them—said, "Luis Tiant, we want you."

He couldn't possibly answer No.

At 8 P.M. that night, just about the time the Beavers and Padres were taking the field before a capacity crowd, Luis made his way to the San Diego airport and boarded a transcontinental flight to New York City.

He arrived at 7 A.M. Saturday, only the second time in his life he had been to this famous metropolis. As the taxi wheeled and lurched through the madness of Manhattan's commuter tieups, Luis gazed out of its windows at the imposing buildings, the faceless masses, and the frenetic pace of everything that moved about him, and more than ever he began to realize just how far he had come from his boyhood days in Nicanor del Campo.

The taxi came to a stop in front of the Biltmore Hotel and Tiant made his way to the room that the Indians had already reserved for him. Once there, he rang Gabe Paul's suite and the general manager asked him to come right over. They shook hands, talked a while and then affixed their signatures to Luis' first big league contract.

That afternoon Tiant accompanied Paul to the ball park where he was ushered into Birdie Tebbetts' office.

"Are you ready to pitch?" Birdie asked.

"Yeh," Luis nodded. "That's what I'm here for. I was supposed to work last night, so I've had five days' rest now."

"Okay," Birdie said. "You're facing Whitey Ford tomorrow."

"Luis Tiant made the sort of major league debut that little boys dream about," wrote Leonard Koppett, leading off his New York *Times* account of Tiant's brilliant 3–0 victory over the Yankees.

Luis had allowed only a bunt single by Tommy Tresh through the first five innings. The fastballs and sliders that had handcuffed opponents in the Pacific Coast League all season long were just as infuriating to the most feared lineup in baseball. Tiant ended up with 11 strikeouts. The Yankees ended up with four scattered singles.

And Whitey Ford, who had come into the game with 12 wins in 14 decisions, ended up with his third loss. "I was good enough to win," he said, "but not against this kid today."

To appreciate the scope of this performance, it's worth noting that on Friday night—while Luis was flying in from San Diego—the Yanks scored seven times in the third inning to clobber Cleveland, 8–4. It was their eighth consecutive victory over the Tribe. Though the Indians managed to break that string on Saturday, winning a 15-inning marathon, New York's ho-hum 6–2 laugher in Sunday's opener seemed to indicate that the water had sought its own level again. And with Ford primed for the nightcap against a freshly graduated Portland Beaver, in the middle of a frantic pennant race to boot, it's a wonder that the crowd of 30,000 bothered to wait for the outcome.

These were still *the* Yankees—the Mantle, Maris, Kubek, Howard Yankees—and they were gunning for their fifth league championship in a row, their ninth in a 10-year span.

And Luis had stopped them cold.

"He was outstanding," Russ Schneider recalls. "He seemed so far ahead of everybody else who came along at that stage."

Luis' prowess only served to fire up a controversy that would irritate him no end. *How old was he?* "I know my first impression of him—based on innuendos, I suppose—was of an old-timer who had been around for quite a while and lied about his age," Schneider smiled. "I was convinced he had knocked about five years off. It just seemed obvious. This was no naïve kid. Luis knew his way around. Plus he even looked older because he was already starting to lose his hair."

Before long he'd begin losing his patience, too, for the repeated references to his *real* age got him madder than a 40-year-old woman who found candles on her cake!

"That's one thing that really upsets him," says Tommy Harper, who knows Luis better than anyone else in baseball. "It started off as a joke, but then it got to a point where everyone seemed to be concerned about his age. And it never let up. Every national publication had to include something about Old Man River. They'd say Luis was 25 going on 32. And he really didn't like it one bit."

Following his great debut, Luis faced the Red Sox five days later and stymied them on six hits, 6–1. Then he sustained his first loss, in Washington, bowing out for a pinch-hitter after limiting the Senators to just three hits in six innings.

Beginning with a 2–1 victory in relief against the Tigers, Tiant continued to roll. A 10-strikeout five-hitter against the Twins and a four-hit shutout of the Angels boosted his record to 5–1.

Minnesota repaid him handsomely a week later, driving him out of the game in the second inning, but Luis' next four decisions were wins, hiking his record to 9–2.

When he beat the pennant-contending White Sox on September 13 in Cleveland, 5–4, he did it by working out of a bases-loaded, one-out jam in the eighth and then retiring the side in order in the ninth.

But he was never better than in his final victory of that rookie season, a 5–0 masterpiece over the Red Sox in Fenway Park, coming right on the heels of Sam McDowell's 3–0 effort in the opener.

The heart of Boston's lineup—Carl Yastrzemski, Tony Conigliaro, George Thomas and Dick Stuart—went 0-for-16 against Tiant's magic. Luis faced only 33 batters, scattering four harmless hits and retiring the final 14 outs in succession.

In the 10½ weeks he'd been with the Indians, the supercool rookie had racked up a 10–4 record, nine complete games, three shutouts and a sparkling 2.83 ERA.

Though the Tribe had another 79–83 record, 20 games behind the Yankees (who edged out Chicago by one game), there was genuine excitement in Cleveland for the first time since Señor Al Lopez—whose six-year regime included one pennant and five second-place finishes—left town in 1956 to take the managerial reins of the White Sox.

Luis, along with McDowell, had given the fans something to think about in the long, cold winter ahead.

CHAPTER 6

The Tiant Motion

I'll try doing anything that I think will help my career. That's the problem with a lot of young kids—pitchers and hitters, too—coming into the big leagues today. They have one big year, then they're washed up.

All through life you should be prepared for something new. Doctors do it, and I think baseball players are no different. After one good year you just can't relax and tell yourself everything will be good from now on. Being good today does not mean you will also be good tomorrow. You've got to keep working at it. Being in the big leagues is not easy.

This is my twelfth year up here, and I'm still trying to find something new to throw at hitters.

—Luis Tiant, 1975

Following the winter season in Puerto Rico, Luis got off to a slow start in the spring of 1965. On May 16 he evened his record at 2–2 with a six-hit victory over the Senators, but that performance was overshadowed by a raging controversy as the Washington players, led by manager Gil Hodges, claimed Tiant was using an illegal motion. American League umpire-in-chief Cal Hubbard promised to investigate.

Five days later another brouhaha erupted in Cleveland when angry Red Sox batters repeated the charge. Eddie Bressoud was so upset at one point that he raced out to second-base umpire Hank Soar to appeal for a second opinion.

"Half the time he throws that changeup, he stops his motion," Boston coach Billy Herman insisted. "It's just like Satchel Paige's old hesitation pitch."

Soar wasn't prepared to go that far, but he did agree that Tiant was worthy of more careful scrutiny.

"He's walking the fine line of a delayed delivery," the veteran official explained to writers who quickly sought him out after the game. "He can come down with his lead foot and delay his arm motion as long as he wants, just so he continues in motion without stopping. It's a very tough pitch, and it's amazing how he can do it just inside the rules and still control it. He's the trickiest pitcher in the league. I can't believe how many pitches and deliveries he's got. He's the only guy I know of who can throw sidearm, crossfire from the stretch, while stepping in the opposite direction."

Then Soar, reflecting on the picture in his mind, broke into a grin. "It's a bit like rubbing your stomach while patting your head with the other hand," he concluded.

Nevertheless, he promised Tiant would be watched very closely.

"If we find he is using a hesitation pitch, we'll allow the man on base to advance. And if no one's on base, we'll call the pitch a ball."

Late one afternoon in June of 1972, as the Red Sox lounged around their clubhouse a few hours before their game against the Tigers, Reggie Smith stood in the center of the room and began a comical pantomime of Luis Tiant on the mound.

Columnist Leigh Montville of the Boston *Globe* was there.

"He was working from the stretch position," Montville wrote, describing Smith. "He was holding an imaginary runner on an imaginary first base, and then he went into his motion. His leg went up, his head bobbed and turned like it was on one of those bubble-headed dolls. His body teetered and tottered and he almost lost his balance. Then he threw, whipping an imaginary fastball from behind his back. *'And that is what I'm waiting for. That's the only damned pitch I've never seen Luis Tiant throw!'"*

As one can see, from the earliest days of his career right through today, people have talked about Tiant's deliveries in terms ranging from anger to amazement to amusement.

"Luis is one of those pitchers, like Sam McDowell, Herb Score, Bob Feller, Nolan Ryan, Sandy Koufax, who can really bother a batter's concentration," Tommy Harper says. "The day before they're due to pitch against you, you're facing someone else, but you're already thinking about *them!*"

Batters discovered that Tiant could do more than just dispatch them with ease. He could also embarrass them, and that possibility was a lot more disarming than the mere concern about striking out.

"I'd rather take my chances against a Ryan any day," Harper said. "You know he's just going to try blowing the ball right past you. He's not going to make you look foolish. But Luis is the type of pitcher everybody hates to go against because he's going to make you look bad up there. He'll have you leaning out on your front foot, then go into his herky-jerky motion and whip a sidearm at you. Or maybe he'll come overhead. Or suddenly change speeds. Or go into his hesitation speed. He's going to get you out, and you're going to look bad doing it. He throws just enough fastballs to keep you honest. And even if you think he's coming in with the off-speed stuff, there aren't too many guys who can stay with it."

The quintessential Tiant motion begins with almost a complete pirouette, so that the batter is left facing the back of Luis' jersey. By itself that's not an insurmountable problem, although it certainly gives the batter an extra concern.

Most pitchers, both the conventional and the nonconventional varieties, have a *spot* the batters can zero in on. It's that precise area where the white of the ball first becomes visible. When you've faced a pitcher enough times you begin to recognize where that spot is, and you instinctively look for it. It seldom varies, no matter what kind of pitch is en route. And if your eye is able to follow the ball from the moment it's released, you usually have time to adjust and react. And that gives you the advantage.

Luis never gives you that advantage.

"He has three, four, maybe five different spots," explains Stan Williams, his teammate in Cleveland and Minnesota and later his pitching coach in Boston. "That's what makes him so unique. If you're up against an overhand pitcher, you just watch for that spot at the top of his delivery—right where his hand comes through—and then follow the ball all the way to the plate. If you can do that, it makes the ball seem like it's coming half speed.

"But nobody knows where the ball's coming from when Luis throws it. One pitch might come sidearm; the next might come at you from three quarters; and then he'll show you an overhand de-livery. On top of all this, Luis has an excellent knack of hiding the ball behind his arm or in his glove. The result is that the batter never sees the pitch until it's almost on top of him."

Carl Yastrzemski—like the legend he replaced in Boston, Ted Williams—has devoted most of his adult life to perfecting his skills at the plate. He does his bit on defense, as his six Golden Glove awards indicate, but nothing in the game of baseball excites him as much as that very personal encounter between the batter and the pitcher.

"I don't think there's any other experience in sports quite like going to the plate to face a pitcher," Yaz explains. "No other situation I can think of reflects so much on the individual. It's just me against him, one-on-one. And that's unique in team sports. Even a field goal kicker needs someone to snap the ball and someone else to hold it. I've had some very great thrills at the plate. I've had some very great disappointments, too."

Like the day he grabbed his bat and went out to face a young Cleveland pitcher named Tiant.

First time up: three fastballs blew right past the letters on his jersey, each emanating from a different point of departure on Tiant's starboard side. Yaz muttered all the way back to the bench.

Second time up: whoosh, whoosh, whoosh! Luis rifled three more fastballs past a now infuriated Yastrzemski, once again em-ploying a full range of spins and gyrations. The Red Sox players were wisely mum as Carl spat out a curse while stomping down the dugout steps.

Third time up: perhaps if Luis had thrown just *one* breaking ball, it might have been interpreted as respect for the threat Yastrzemski represented. But all Yaz got was blistering heat. And it burned him a third time. If you've ever seen Yastrzemski's home run swing, you know it can be gracious and vicious at once. But now it had been reduced to a desperate lunge as Carl frantically lashed out at Luis' final offering, almost toppling over from the sheer exertion of the effort. And, as Harper warned, he looked bad.

"Speed, plain speed, doesn't usually bother hitters," Carl says. "At least I know it doesn't bother me. But Luis comes at you from all angles and throws your timing off. There's no zone you can look for and *know* that's where the ball will be coming from. The guy who is herky-jerky, who can completely hide the ball and then deliver it at the last split second, he's the guy who bothers you most of all. Luis is the only guy I can think of who kept me guessing every minute."

And how about looking bad?

"Looking bad?" Yaz repeated. "If you strike out, what the hell's the difference?"

One might wonder why—instead of bitching and moaning about the alleged impropriety of his pitches—opponents didn't simply follow suit and jump aboard the bandwagon until, at last, the entire American League pitching corps was rocking and reeling like a flashback to a sock hop of the fifties.

Perhaps for the very same reason NBA opponents didn't just decide to rebound the way Bill Russell did, and NHL foes don't just decide to skate the way Bobby Orr does.

"Someone else could walk out there and try to do the same things Luis does," Stan Williams noted, "and he'd have no success at all. You see, the motion is just a part of what makes Luis so special. What a lot of people overlook is the fact he has an excellent knowledge of his trade. He's a complete professional. He knows how to set up hitters, how to move the ball around, how to change speeds at the right time, how to pitch to a hitter's weakness. All of these things are so important. But most important of all is the fact that Luis has A-1 excellent control. He can throw that ball within an inch or two of where he wants it, and he can do it continually, pitch after pitch after pitch."

So if he's that clever, why go into all of his extraneous exhibitions of flamenco dancing on the hill? Why not stick to pure pitching?

There are those who contend Tiant is a bit of a hot dog, a bit of a ham.

Harper and Williams are not among them.

"It's hard to draw a line between being a hot dog and being a showman," Stan feels. "But I'd prefer to call Luis' style showmanship. He doesn't do all of these extra things for the same reason a hot dog would do them. He's one of the funniest people I've ever met—I used to call him the Cuban Cantinflas—but once Luis walks across that line, he's all business. Everything he does is for the express purpose of getting the batter out. Sure, maybe now and then he'll give an extra head toss just to excite the fans, but his main idea is still to deceive the hitter. And if you watch some of the swings they take, you'll see it's all quite effective."

"He's not a hot dog in the way players use the term," Harper concurs. "He doesn't fit into that category at all. I've never heard of any hitter resenting Luis, or going back to the dugout complaining that Luis was trying to show him up. The man's just tough to hit and everybody knows it."

Indeed, ballplayers have come to marvel at Tiant's special genius, just as surely as the customers have been known to oooh and aaah whenever he's at work.

"Luis doesn't have a pitcher's body," observes Red Sox southpaw star Bill Lee. "He's like Pete Rose in that respect; he makes the best of limited tools. He has a stocky-type frame, whereas the majority of great pitchers—Sandy Koufax, Nolan Ryan, Vida Blue—have pure athletes' bodies. I look at the way Luis winds up and goes through all of those gyrations, and sometimes it hurts me to watch him throw. But I'm always amazed by his concentration and desire. He gives everything he's got to winning."

Those early-season furors were only harbingers of what was to come. Toward the end of the 1965 campaign Luis—ever on the alert to find "something new"—startled writers and fans alike, not to mention opposing batters, when he unveiled his latest contortion.

"I call it the 'jaw breaker,' " he told reporters from behind a cloud of cigar smoke.

"Can you explain it, Luis?" a columnist requested.

"Sure," Tiant grinned. "My head stops seven times. Once it looks up; once it looks down; once it points the jaw at second base; once it points it to third; once it points it at the scoreboard; once it points to behind my back; and then just before I let go of the ball, it points the jaw upstairs to where Gabe Paul is sitting."

Clearly, the writer got what he asked for.

CHAPTER 7

Starring in Mudville

The seasons of 1965, 1966 and 1967 can at once be reviewed together, and then forgotten together, for baseball in Cleveland was truly that monotonous.

"It just wasn't fun," Russ Schneider remembers. "We were never favored to win anything, yet we were always competitive. What it amounted to was that we were just good enough to finish in the middle. Oh, there was always some promise: a guy like Tiant or McDowell, or a real good rookie like Max Alvis . . . there was always someone who was going to step in and save the franchise by helping us to win a pennant."

Saving the franchise was not a figurative way of putting it, for very serious thought had been given to pulling the Indians out of Cleveland and beating Charley Finley to what was later recognized as fool's gold in Oakland.

Vernon Stouffer, head of the food corporation that bears his surname, was the restless owner of the Tribe in those dog days of the mid-sixties, and perhaps one couldn't blame him for entertaining visions of greener pastures.

The city belonged to the Browns. Everybody knew that. This

had been Jimmy Brown's town from the day he arrived in 1957 until the day he left for Hollywood in 1965.

And, as luck would have it, the Browns' finest hours were concurrent with the Tribe's era of tedium.

The 1964 Indians finished sixth, two games under .500. Then the Browns opened shop and went 10–3–1 before downing the Colts, 27–0, for the NFL championship.

The 1965 Indians finished fifth, six games over .500. Then along came the Browns with an 11–3 record and another appearance in the championship game (which they lost to Green Bay).

The 1966 Indians were also fifth, this time with exactly a .500 record (81–81). And the Browns followed that with a 9–5 season.

By 1967 the Indians had slumped to eighth, six games under the .500 level. But the Browns were still flying high, winning their divisional crown.

Little wonder, therefore, that Stouffer seriously contemplated an invitation to pack the club's bags and take up residence in Seattle, one of several cities which were clamoring for a major league team.

"Twice during those years we came very close to losing the franchise," Schneider reflected. "In fact, we started a big 'Save the Indians' campaign in the newspaper. There was very little to cheer about."

Rocky Colavito led the league in RBI in 1965, and McDowell won a pair of strikeout titles, along with the ERA crown once, but otherwise Cleveland sort of resembled Mudville before Casey came to bat.

Luis, meanwhile, continued to establish himself as one of the league's blossoming stars, even though he was forced to operate in the shadows of the team's anonymity.

Following that celebrated win over Washington in early 1965, the one in which his motion caused such a stir, he won his next three decisions for a mid-June record of 5–2. Two of those victories came against the White Sox, the league's second-best team. The third triumph was a brilliant two-hitter against the pennant-bound Twins, who had been averaging more than five runs a game with their monstrous lineup of Tony Oliva, Harmon Killebrew and Bob Allison. It was only the fourth complete game against

Minnesota, and it cost Jim Grant a 2–1 defeat, even though he had limited the Indians to just five hits.

"Luis has about 10 different pitches," Grant said, shaking his head, "and he can get every one of them in there for a strike."

After a bad outing against Kansas City, Tiant reeled off another four wins in a row, beginning with a one-hit, 5–0 thing of beauty against the Senators in which he recorded seven strikeouts. Through six innings the excitement of a potential no-hitter continued to escalate; then Woody Held broke the spell by stroking a clean single to open the seventh.

"I've got to make a living, too," Woody reminded reporters.

On August 11, Luis had a 10–5 record.

Then he lost six of his final seven decisions to end the season at 11–11, but that dreadful tailspin bears closer inspection.

He went eight innings against the Twins, allowing just three hits and a walk, but Cleveland bowed, 4–3.

Five days later he went 8⅓ innings against the Senators, fanning nine and walking two. Cleveland lost, 3–2.

But the nadir of his 1965 frustrations probably came on a mid-September day in Boston when, with an 11–10 record and a winning season at stake, he threw a two-hitter at the Red Sox, striking out 11, *and lost, 2–0!*

"I don't care how well you pitch," he shrugged on his way to the whirlpool tank. "If you get no runs, you get no wins."

When Luis arrived at the 1966 training camp, he startled Birdie Tebbetts and his teammates with his new look. Troubled by his son's mediocre record and photos he had seen, Señor Tiant wrote Luis a letter at the conclusion of the 1965 schedule.

"He told me to get skinny," Luis smiles.

Tiant heeded the advice and showed up the following spring weighing 20 pounds less and boasting a waistline that had shrunk two inches.

The writers converged on him.

"At first I couldn't lose anything," he explained. "The diet the doctor gave me almost killed me! I couldn't eat anything, and I still couldn't lose anything. So I started exercising and went on my own diet. My wife wouldn't give me any more fried food—only boiled and broiled. And she wouldn't let me eat any bread. She kept telling me no candy, no soda, no eating at night. She even exercised with me."

Then he laughed.

"But she didn't lose any weight!"

Luis kicked off his season with three consecutive shutouts in which he piled up 25 strikeouts (against eight walks) in 27 innings.

His bid for a fourth was dramatically terminated in Baltimore as Frank Robinson got behind a low-and-inside pitch and drove it clear out of Memorial Stadium in the first inning. The ball—the only one ever hit out of that park—traveled 451 feet on the fly and was eventually recovered by two teen-agers who located it underneath a parked car, *540 feet away from home plate!* That earned Robinson a tremendous standing ovation from the 49,516 partisans on hand when he took the field to begin the second inning.

Tiant's fourth win did come via a shutout, however, with him stopping the Tigers on four hits. The game was highlighted by a tense duel that saw Willie Horton work the count to 3–2 with two men on and two men out in the seventh. With both squads squirming on their dugout steps, Tiant fired seven strikes; Horton fouled off six of them, then went down swinging on the seventh, ending a minidrama that lasted six minutes.

"Can that man fire!" Willie exclaimed later. "The worst part is trying to figure which direction the ball's going to come from. It's like facing four pitchers all at once."

Luis smiled at that.

"Tell him he's like facing four batters at once. I had to strike him out four times to get him out of there!"

In his next start Luis went eight innings against the Twins, fanned seven, walked one and yielded three hits, but Minnesota beat him, 1–0.

Then he appeared to go sour, lasting no more than five innings in any of his next eight appearances.

"I felt good after losing that weight," he remembers, "but when we came north it was cold, and when it's cold you don't sweat that much. That bothered me. By the time it got warm, I began getting tired after two or three innings. There was nothing wrong with my arm; I was just tired and weak."

On July 6 he was sent to the bullpen, where he would remain for most of the balance of the season, making 25 appearances in relief.

"Remember when Luis Tiant had the American League buzzing about the three straight shutouts he pitched early in the season?" sportswriter Jim Hennemen asked his readers one morning in July. "Well, you can forget about it, because the bulky, flame-throwing right-hander isn't likely to get the chance to do it again for a while."

One of his first relief appearances came against the Orioles, who were already leaving the rest of the field in their dust. Luis pitched 2⅔ innings, striking out three and giving up no hits and no walks, but someone else got the victory. That took some getting used to.

On September 18 he went 2⅓ innings against the high-scoring Tigers, recording five strikeouts against no hits and no walks. That earned him his ninth win, along with his release from captivity. George Strickland, who had replaced Tebbetts in August, told Luis he was going back into the starting rotation.

Tiant won his next three starts, including a 12-strikeout gem against the Twins, which he won 4–1; an easy 3–1 decision over the Athletics; and a return engagement against the Twins, whom he shut out, 4–0.

In his final appearance of the season, Luis went the distance against the Angels, striking out seven, walking none, and scattering four hits. Cleveland lost, 2–0. It seemed a grimly appropriate note to end the 1966 campaign with.

Over the course of 155 innings, he had compiled a respectable 2.79 ERA, and his strikeouts (145) almost tripled his walks allowed (50). But all anybody was going to remember was that he had been a 12–11 pitcher on a .500 team.

Luis got off to a magnificent start in 1967.

He fanned nine Senators in his first victory, a 3–1 decision in Washington that evened his record at 1–1. Then he struck out nine Red Sox, but failed to get a decision after more than six innings of three-hit pitching. He continued to roll, however: there was a 9–1 win over Washington with 12 strikeouts; a 9–0 whitewash of Detroit with 13 strikeouts (giving him 43 strikeouts in four games!).

The Twins cooled him off temporarily with a barrage of five homers, but he quickly regained his stride.

In his next three outings he struck out 11 in a 12–1 laugher over the A's; fanned nine in a 2–1, 10-inning struggle against the Twins; and whiffed seven in another triumph over Kansas City.

That gave him six winning decisions in a row.

But there was no escaping the fact that he played for Cleveland. In Tiant and "Sudden Sam" McDowell, the Indians had two of baseball's premier young pitching talents, one who delivered from the right and the other who worked from the left. They should have been a formidable pair.

Sam, however, would finish second in the league in strikeouts (236) and wind up with a 13–15 record.

Luis would finish fourth in the league in strikeouts (219) and close out at 12–9, despite a 2.73 ERA.

"Those had to be frustrating years for Luis," Russ Schneider says. "No one ever took the Indians seriously because everyone knew they'd be out of the race by the end of July. The best example was 1966. We started off winning 14 out of 15 and finished up in fifth place. It just wasn't an encouraging atmosphere to work in."

When Luis stopped the Tigers on June 29 by a 5–3 score (only one run earned), his record was 7–2. In a dozen starts he had notched 93 strikeouts, or an average of nearly eight per game.

Then he lost six in a row.

They included a 10-strikeout three-hitter against Detroit (2–1) and a seven-strikeout two-hitter against New York (4–1, three Yankee runs unearned).

When he finally won again on August 22, he had to strike out 16 Angels before securing a 3–2 verdict that evened his record at 8–8.

In September Luis bowed out as dramatically as he had entered back in springtime, winning his final four appearances in which he chalked up 36 more strikeouts.

But once again there was no real cause for elation as he headed back to Mexico City, at least not as far as baseball was concerned.

There was a great deal of excitement back home, however, when Maria gave birth to their first daughter—Isabel—on October 14. Luis, who had been away in Charleston, South Carolina, when little Luis arrived, was able to be with his wife this time, and for the next month or so they simply sat back and enjoyed themselves as a family.

Then Luis packed up and headed for Venezuela and some more winter ball. He surely had no reason to suspect that 1968 in Cleveland would be much different than 1965, 1966 or 1967 had been.

PART III
Heights and Depths

CHAPTER 8

A Beautiful Friendship

Somewhere along the line from Topeka, where his pro career began in 1960, to Cincinnati, where he spent five seasons, Tommy Harper acquired a reputation as a moody, sullen sort of guy. Reporters generally steered clear of him, having heard he was a loner. Those who disregarded the grapevine and took the bother to seek him out discovered Tommy was not only willing to talk baseball with them, but was actually warm and friendly when drawn out of his shell. Given his choice, however, Harper preferred leaving the limelight to his more illustrious mates like Vada Pinson, Frank Robinson and Pete Rose.

In November of 1967, the Reds traded Tommy to Cleveland. He didn't have any special emotions over the deal. Cleveland didn't mean much to him, and Luis Tiant was little more than a name he occasionally tripped across on the sports pages. But now their paths were destined to cross at spring training, 1968.

By then Luis had a well-deserved image as a clubhouse cutup, a guy who'd go to ridiculous lengths just to get a laugh.

"He was a very funny man," Russ Schneider smiles. "He would do anything to make a joke succeed, and I often wondered why he never got hurt. He did some crazy things."

Luis was always careful to pick the proper targets for his pranks. There are players who just wouldn't see the hilarity in having someone crawl across the clubhouse floor to light a match under a newspaper they were reading.

"Before I go fooling with people," Luis explains, "I study them. I think I'm pretty good at that. That's why no one gets mad at me. Before I do anything to someone, I make sure I know what his reaction will be."

A few days after the Tribe assembled in March, Harper took it upon himself to make the rounds of the locker room, introducing himself to the men he'd be living with for the next seven months.

"He came over to me," Luis recalls, "shook my hand and said hello. But he was very quiet about it. I liked him right away. I had heard from other players that Tommy was a good man. So we started talking, and he became my friend."

In those first few days Harper discovered that Tiant—pranks and wisecracks notwithstanding—had a heavy heart that he seldom unburdened among friends. But Tommy soon learned about the mother and father in Cuba, about the wife and two children in Mexico City, and he began to see through the laughing major leaguer to the melancholy man inside.

"I just liked Luis from the beginning," Tommy remembers. "Maybe the fact he had no family with him made me want to show him that things still weren't so bad here in this country. We talked about it a little bit. I guess I wanted him to know he didn't have to go looking for a country, or looking for a home. At least by me being a good friend, I figured he'd always have someone he could talk with, someone he could count on if he needed something. It wouldn't be as if he was completely alone, with no one close to him until the season was over."

And so it was that the seeds of a very beautiful friendship were sown that spring in Tucson, Arizona.

But Tommy was still the quiet man in the clubhouse, just as he'd always been, and his daily routine rarely varied. He'd walk into the room, murmur a few hellos or perhaps simply nod in recognition, then dress quickly and head out onto the field. No fanfare, no commotion, no fuss. Indeed, he was as inconspicuous as the proverbial church mouse.

And Luis didn't fail to notice this.

So one day, as Tommy walked past him on his way to his locker, Luis jumped up. "Whew!!" he grimaced, pointing an accusing finger at Harper. *"Alligator breath!"*

Up and down the rows of lockers heads turned to see what the noise was all about.

By now Luis was gagging. *"Alligator breath!"* he moaned. *"I'm dying."*

As the Indians burst into hysterics, Harper just stood and stared in disbelief at the death scene that truly belonged in the final act of *Hamlet*.

He was understandably shaken. Dressing hurriedly, he made a hasty exit. The next day he arrived with apprehension, not quite sure what he had done to trigger such an incident, but damned sure he wasn't going to do a thing that might bring on a repeat performance. One can well imagine Tommy's relief, therefore, as he walked into the clubhouse and discovered Luis wasn't there. He released a grateful sigh and started on his way to his locker.

"EEEEEAAAAAIIIII!"

The scream reverberated throughout the room, and Tommy felt a growing sense of panic as he turned around.

He saw the bright red fireman's hat before he saw the familiar face beneath it.

"EEEEEAAAAAIIIII," Luis wailed as he screeched to a halt, hoisted a fire extinguisher, and slipped its nozzle into Harper's open mouth.

"No more *alligator breath!*" he triumphantly shouted as he withdrew the nozzle, spun around, and raced out of the room. "EEEEEAAAAAIIIII!"

Harper watched him disappear around a corner, then surveyed the room of laughing Indians and began to laugh himself. Soon Luis returned and everyone was howling.

"It was the first time that anyone had really put me under a spotlight," Tommy says. "The people in Cincinnati understood that I'm a quiet person, so they just let me be. But Luis never let me alone. It seemed I became the butt of every joke in his book. It's funny, but I really didn't mind it. In fact, it kind of made me feel good."

CHAPTER 9

The 21-Victory Season

As the 1968 season got under way the American League was still feeling the effects of the magnificent 1967 race, an historic down-to-the-wire struggle that saw Boston, by virtue of a final-day victory over the Twins, win the pennant by a one-game margin over Minnesota and Detroit. The Twins and Tigers had been expected to make serious runs for the flag, but Boston literally came from nowhere, having finished ninth in 1966. The Red Sox' dramatic surge was tonic for all the downtrodden, an Horatio Alger epic coming to life before the eyes of a spellbound audience that stretched from one coast to the other.

The message was clear: *every day is a new beginning, a chance to start all over and get it right.*

But could the 1968 Indians really believe that? Was the so-called "Impossible Dream" in Boston only a mirage, or could they, too, aspire to greater heights as they broke camp and prepared to venture onto their 162-game odyssey? New manager Alvin Dark assured them it was so, but it remained for Luis to get that point across by example.

After absorbing an early loss in relief, Luis got his first starting assignment and stymied the White Sox, 3–1, on a four-hitter, fanning nine.

The Red Sox stopped him once, then he began to roll:

• Washington, 2–0, a two-hitter, seven strikeouts;
• Minnesota, 4–0, a three-hitter, nine strikeouts;
• New York, 8–0, a five-hitter, 10 strikeouts;
• Baltimore, 2–0, a four-hitter, nine strikeouts.

"We used to give a suit to anybody pitching a shutout," Gabe Paul smiles. "It wasn't long before Luis was the best-dressed man in town."

The four consecutive shutouts gave him a 5–2 record.

After dropping a pair to Baltimore (a nine-strikeout four-hitter) and Oakland (2–0), Luis got rolling again:

• California, 5–2, a four-hitter, 12 strikeouts;
• Washington, 8–3;
• Chicago, 2–1, a four-hitter;
• Detroit, 2–0, a four-hitter.

The four consecutive wins hiked his record to 9–4, and it was still only the ninth of June.

Boston put the brakes on Tiant's streak, though he recorded 10 strikeouts in bowing to the Red Sox.

And then he resumed his one-man rampage by winning his next seven games in a row giving him an overall stretch of 11 wins in 12 tries.

It began with a three-hitter against the White Sox, 3–1.

Then Luis earned a couple of spots in the record book with his next three appearances. The first was a three-hit shutout against Detroit in which he struck out nine; the second was an 8–1 win over Boston, in which he fanned 13!

And, finally, his *pièce de résistance,* maybe the finest game he ever pitched in his life. It came on a Wednesday night in Cleveland, the eve of the Fourth of July, and more than 21,000 fans had come to Municipal Stadium to watch Luis, now 12–5, try his magic on the Twins. His opponent would be Jim Merritt, and Merritt would go on to pitch brilliantly.

"At a time when they received a pitching masterpiece from one of their own," Dwayne Netland told the home folks in the next morning's edition of the Minneapolis *Tribune,* "the Twins had the supreme misfortune to encounter one of the finest pitchers in baseball having the greatest night of his career."

Through nine innings the game remained scoreless and Merritt —as Netland observed—was superb, allowing the Indians only two singles: a two-out shot by Duke Sims in the second, and Joe Azcue's safety in the seventh.

The Twins, meanwhile, were having just as much trouble with Tiant, whose fastball was virtually untouchable. Their only threat had come in the sixth when Cesar Tovar opened with a double, but it immediately died when Tovar tried to stretch it into a triple and was gunned down on a perfect relay.

And the end of nine innings, Luis had 16 strikeouts!

But in the tenth it appeared he was at last vulnerable. Rich Reese hammered his first pitch for a double, and Frank Quilici followed with a perfectly executed sacrifice bunt. Sims, hoping to nail the advancing Reese, fired to third, but he was too late. Now Luis was faced with runners on second and third, and no outs:

John Roseboro worked him to a 3–1 count; then Tiant blew two fastballs past his letters for his seventeenth strikeout.

Luis needed only four pitches to make pinch-hitter Rich Rollins his eighteenth strikeout victim.

And then he disposed of Merritt on just three pitches, killing the threat and walking off the field with his nineteenth strikeout.

"The fans arose as one with an ovation—the likes of which has not been heard in the Stadium for years," Russ Schneider reported.

The 19 Ks were an American League record for a 10-inning game, and just two shy of the 21 strikeouts Tom Cheney threw for Washington in a 16-inning affair in 1962, the all-time single-game high.

In addition, they gave Luis 41 strikeouts in three games, another American League record.

But it all would have been for naught if the Indians hadn't finally pushed a run across in the home half of the tenth when Lou Johnson hit an infield single, took second on a throwing error and raced home with an unearned run when Azcue singled to right.

Luis was mobbed by admiring teammates, fans and writers.

"That's got to be the top performance I've ever seen under these conditions," Dark raved. "He had to work under a handicap. It looked as though we'd never score a run for him. I've seen many great jobs, but the way he had to do it tonight was the greatest."

Even home plate umpire Ed Runge was tossing bouquets at Tiant.

"I can't say enough about that performance," he marveled. "He's a great pitcher. Every time I've seen him this year he's been great. Whenever he got into trouble tonight he just reared back and fired. He challenged them all night long."

When all of the statistics were sorted it was revealed that Luis had thrown 135 pitches, *and 101 had been strikes!*

Appropriately, Tiant was given the starting assignment the following week in Houston when the American League All-Stars squared off against their National League counterparts. In what was to become symbolic of his 1968 season, Luis lost the game when Willie Mays scored on a double-play ball in the first inning. The final score was 1–0.

Following the All-Star break, Luis won three in a row, completing that string of seven straight and 11 out of 12.

Then Baltimore beat him, 1–0.

Tiant rebounded with a 10-strikeout five-hitter against New York, jacking his record to 17–6; then lost to Baltimore; then went nine innings against Detroit, yielding just four hits, without a decision.

The Indians simply weren't hitting for him, and the victories were coming harder and harder.

On August 10 he finally won his eighteenth, holding Chicago to five hits while striking out 10.

Then the Tigers came to town and Luis struck out nine, walked none, and lost to Denny McLain, 3–0.

It was Denny's twenty-fourth win in 27 decisions, keeping him on a pace that would eventually bring him 31 victories and a unanimous vote for the Cy Young Award.

"Luis and I would each be fighting for 30 wins if he had our kind of hitting to go with his kind of pitching," McLain advised writers after the game. "I've been getting more than five runs a game to work with. If I just stay close to the other team I have a 99 per cent chance of winning. If he stays close, he's got a 50-50 chance."

Luis wasn't the only guy affected by Cleveland's power failure. Sam McDowell would lead the league in strikeouts and post a 1.81 ERA, second only to Tiant's, yet wind up with a 15–14 record.

"If Luis played for us," Tiger catcher Bill Freehan insisted, "he'd be shooting for 40 wins."

Tiant accepted the platitudes with a futile shrug. "Maybe they're right," he said. "I don't know. All I know is that I'm not a Tiger. I'm an Indian. So all I want is 20 wins."

But the goal was looking increasingly difficult. His record was now 18–8. In seven of those losses the Tribe gave him fewer than three runs to work with. In 12 of his 26 overall decisions he received two runs or less to work with. And in a dozen instances the Cleveland lineup didn't produce its first run until at least the sixth inning!

"Luis has an unbelievable record right now," manager Dark pointed out. "Considering what this team has given him for support, he's been positively fantastic."

Five days later he tried again for No. 19, allowing the Red Sox five hits. He lost, 3–0.

Then he pitched two-hit ball against the Senators for five innings, got lifted for a pinch-hitter and, as a result, was not around to pick up credit for Cleveland's 2–1 triumph.

Four days later he went out to face the Twins, holding them to two hits through five innings. Then his elbow stiffened and he couldn't go any farther. He stomped off the mound in disgust, but at least he left with a 2–1 lead. Then reliever Vicente Romo gave up the tying run. The Indians scored once more, and Romo was proclaimed the 3–2 winner.

"I never have an easy inning," Luis fumed in the trainer's room. "I must throw hard all the time, and this puts a strain on my elbow. I've had only two easy games all year. If I give up one run I feel I'm going to lose the game. That's too hard on my arm. Too hard."

Ironically, after four grand attempts at No. 19 failed, Luis picked up the elusive victory in California with one of his worst efforts of the year, winning 9–5 after being shelled in the sixth!

Five days later he won his celebrated twentieth against the Twins, the same team he recorded 19 strikeouts against in July. This time he struck out 16!

And for a very fitting finale, Luis completed his season by shutting out the Yankees, 3–0, on a one-hitter with 11 strikeouts. The only New York hit was Mickey Mantle's grounder through the infield in the first.

Tiant ended up with a 21–9 record, the most wins for any Indian since Early Wynn and Bob Lemon notched 23 apiece in the pennant year of 1954. He also had an ERA of 1.60, lowest in the American League since Walter (Big Train) Johnson's 1.49 in 1919!

"Luis was the best pitcher in the league that year," says Stan Williams, his teammate that summer and one of his best friends. "Yeh, Denny won 31, but if anyone had asked me which one was the better player, I'd have taken Luis 100 times in a row. We have a little saying; it's called 'bowing your neck.' It means getting a little tougher when the situation is tougher. Some pitchers can do and some can't. Luis could. Like that night he struck out 19, including three in the tenth with men in scoring position. Luis is as good a man as you'll ever want to see with someone on third and nobody out. He'll 'bow his neck,' so to speak. He'll reach back and find that little something extra, just like he did that night against the Twins."

It was an opinion widely shared.

"The one thing I'll always remember about Tiant in 1968 was that he was such a bulldog, such a fierce competitor," Schneider said. "If he went into the sixth or seventh with any kind of a lead, forget it. Luis was *not* going to lose that ball game. Gabe Paul used to say 'his nostrils flared like a bull' or something like that, and for a while the radio guys began referring to him as 'the little bull.' He was such a determined guy. He always seemed to be reaching for that something extra that nobody else could get. That characterized him in my mind, along, of course, with his marvelous sense of humor."

So Luis should have been sitting on top of the world when the 1968 campaign came to a close.

But that's not the way the story went.

In the game against Minnesota that saw Tiant withdraw because of a stiffness in his elbow, a simmering controversy was brought to a boil.

Alvin Dark never liked the idea of Tiant's many motions on the mound. Dark was a meat and potatoes man when it came to baseball. He didn't appreciate anything he perceived to be frivolous or unnecessary, and yet he had to bite his tongue where Luis was concerned. As long as Luis kept winning it was impossible to criticize his methods.

But now Tiant had pulled himself out of a game, complaining of soreness, and Alvin seized the moment to raise the issue that had been festering all summer long.

"I've always believed his extreme motions had to put a strain somewhere," he told writers. "I don't think he needs all of those motions. All he has to do is throw hard. He'll just take years off of his career if he keeps throwing this way."

Tiant was indignant. In his last 23 innings, covering four appearances, the Indians had given him exactly *two* runs! Both Sonny Siebert and Steve Hargan had preceded him as sore-armed members of the Cleveland staff, and Luis was adamant about the reason why.

"Motions don't hurt my arm," he informed reporters who had read Dark's quotes to him. "No runs. That's what hurts my arm. It started hurting a week ago, but I kept pitching. Four times I tried to win No. 19, and four times I got no runs. Still I kept pitching, hoping maybe I can win 20. Now the pain is up to my elbow."

One could make a case for either side.

The night Luis lost to McLain, Al Kaline observed, "He's got to hurt his arm throwing that way. He won't have a long career."

But Cleveland pitching coach Jack Sanford agreed that much of the problem stemmed from the continuous pressure Luis had to deal with. "He's pitched so hard all year that I'm not surprised he's hurting now," Sanford said. "Every pitch has had to be a big pitch, and no arm can take that for long. I can't remember the last time Luis had a breather or an easy game to work."

After missing two starts, Luis returned to beat California and Minnesota for his nineteenth and twentieth wins, both coming on the road. Back in Cleveland he was due to face Baltimore in his next start, but as he warmed up in the bullpen, his arm began to throb. Finally he told catcher Ken Suarez to inform Dark he couldn't pitch that night. Rookie Steve Bailey was named as a last-minute substitute and he took a pounding from the powerful Orioles.

In the next morning's papers Dark said he was "surprised" that Tiant would quit before the game started.

Luis was furious. He stormed into the manager's office and flung the paper across the desk, hitting Alvin in the chest with it.

"Look," he seethed, "I'm the only pitcher you've got on your staff here who never gives you any shit. I just come in here every day and pitch. I know that's the only way I'm going to make any money. I never come in here with excuses. You should know that better than I do. The rest of these guys are always getting dizzy or having colds or not feeling good, but you never say anything in the papers about them. Why did you have to say this about me?"

"You're taking it the wrong way," Dark said.

"I don't care what way I'm taking it," Tiant retorted. "You're not supposed to say those things about your players in the papers. I do my job for you and for this ball club, so I should be respected. You never hear any excuses from me, but I've been pitching with a sore elbow and you know it."

Dark began to respond.

"Never mind," Tiant snapped. "From now on, if I don't feel good, I don't pitch. I don't care if you get mad, or if you trade me, or whatever else happens. If I'm not 100 per cent, I don't pitch."

Dark protested that Luis misunderstood his remarks.

"That's your problem," Luis replied, walking out the door. "I just came in here to tell you how I feel, face to face, like a man."

It was 12 days before Luis worked again, striking out five in a two-inning stint and getting no decision. Then came that one-hitter in his curtain call against the Yankees, his twenty-first and final victory.

He planned to visit with Maria, little Luis and Isabel for a while before moving on to Venezuela where he had spent the past three winters playing ball.

But then the Indians told him they would not allow him to play any more until the following spring.

"That really got Luis mad," Schneider remembers. "He was our Man of the Year at the baseball writers dinner that winter, and he told me that night he was afraid that missing winter ball was going to hurt him. He said his arm would stiffen and his muscles would shorten, and, you know, all of that jazz these fellows usually talk about. And I remember him saying he was going to make the Indians pay for the money he would lose, both the money he wouldn't get in winter ball and the salary he'd probably lose by having a bad season in 1969. I sort of ignored it at the time, figuring, you know, he was just another ballplayer looking for an angle. But he did forecast what was going to happen in 1969."

CHAPTER 10

A Surprise Visit

The frequent phone calls from Luis to his parents were always concluded with mixed emotions. While it was good to talk with them again, to be brought up to date on happenings back home and to tell them everything they wanted to know about the grandchildren they had never seen, the goodbyes invariably left him heartsick, for they only served to underscore his tremendous sense of loss and to fan anew his hidden fears that he'd never see or embrace either parent again.

A particularly painful call followed his appearance in the 1968 All-Star Game. His mother, it seemed, had been able to watch the game in a friend's home, and later she told Luis what it had been like, sitting there, staring at the image of the only child she bore, the boy she hadn't held or kissed for more than seven years now.

"I watched you on the television," she said, "and all the while I watched I cried because I wanted to reach out and touch you and I couldn't."

Luis cried, too, as he listened.

Though Maria Tiant didn't say so, being aware of her husband's irritation over the ruling, she was secretly pleased that Luis wouldn't be going to Venezuela or anyplace else this winter. Since their marriage in 1961, home had been little more than a stopping point on his way north to south each fall, and south to north each spring. He was a good husband, she reminded herself, and a doting father, and all she and the children could ask for was to see more of him.

Now, for the first time, they'd have a whole winter together.

It was an arrangement that soon pleased Luis, too, for little Luis was now six years old and Isabel was almost one. These were years to cherish, he realized, for they'd pass all too soon, and if they were lost they could never be retrieved.

As September faded into October the pace picked up. The holiday season was fast approaching, but even before that there was Isabel's birthday to celebrate.

On October 14 the cake and goodies and presents were all assembled for the party that evening, but now Luis had a few hours to himself for relaxation, so he invited a friend over to watch the Olympics with him on television. They were having a good time, sharing wine, laughs and camaraderie while watching the pageantry on the screen, and he really didn't hear his sister-in-law, Concepcion, enter the room.

"Hey," she said, poking Luis on the shoulder, "do you remember this?"

He turned in his chair to see her standing beside an old, battered suitcase.

"No," he said, a bit impatiently, as he turned back to watch the games.

"Are you sure?" she asked.

He turned once more, gave another cursory inspection to the scruffy old valise and shook his head.

"I never saw it before," he said, dismissing the subject.

Concepcion persisted.

"Look some more," she said.

Luis was becoming agitated. He got out of his chair and walked over to the case, and this time he really studied it, but it still didn't ring any bells in his mind. As he started back to his chair he noticed the door to the hallway was open.

"I looked out," he remembers, "and my mother was standing there hugging Maria."

In an instant Luis was standing in the hallway with them, sobbing uncontrollably as he wrapped his mother in his arms.

She closed her eyes and cupped his face in her hands.

"Why are you crying?" she joked softly. "I'm the one who should cry."

Luis didn't answer. He just held on and wept.

In the months that followed, Christmastime in particular, Luis hardly thought of baseball. He was fully immersed in family life as the son, the husband and the father in that happy Mexico City apartment. But at the end of January the inevitable hour of decision had arrived for Señora Tiant. She had loved Maria as a daughter from the moment they met, and the children had brought her unsurpassed joy. It was almost like being permitted to relive—just for a moment—those treasured years when the home in Nicanor del Campo was filled with the sounds of life, when Juanito and Abelardo and Jorgito would come calling for Luis, when friends stopped by to eat and drink and laught, when there was no reason to suspect that all of their tomorrows would be any different from their todays.

But that must have been a million years ago.

Her little boy was now a man with children of his own, living in an altogether different world, a world she so desperately longed to share in whatever years were left for her.

Luis asked her to stay. So did Maria. So did little Luis.

And so did Señor Tiant in a heartrending call from Cuba. He told his wife to remain in Mexico City with their son, to build her life around his, to recapture as much as she could of what had been taken away from her.

But she said No, just as Luis knew she would.

"I can't leave your father alone," she explained, "not after all of our years together."

Luis nodded.

"If that's what's in your heart," he said, "then go."

Years later their tearful farewell remained indelibly etched in his mind.

"It hurt so badly to let her go," he said. "But I didn't want her to stay if she'd end up so sad and lonely that it would kill her."

So they drove her to the airport, kissed her goodbye and watched the plane as it flew out of sight, en route to an old man in Cuba who'd be waiting to hear every bit of the news she carried with her.

CHAPTER 11

Collision Course

In 1969 the major leagues expanded. Two new franchises came into the American League: Seattle (which acquired Tommy Harper in the expansion draft) and Kansas City, which had lost its Athletics to Oakland the year before. As a result the league was divided into two six-team divisions, both of which would send their first-place teams into a championship playoff series to determine who would represent the circuit in the World Series.

But all of this maneuvering had very little meaning in Cleveland. The Indians (62–99) finished sixth in the American League East. If the league had remained one big undivided field they would have finished twelfth.

The situation would have been depressing enough in the best of times, but in 1969 it seemed especially cruel to those fans who believed the third-place finish of 1968 was an accurate reflection of their team's abilities.

It was not.

"In 1968 we got every bit of talent out of everybody who was there," Russ Schneider explains. "In other words, we couldn't possibly have done any better than we did. Finishing third was one great achievement. It was not a situation where anybody could say, 'Jesus, if so-and-so had done such-and-such we might have finished higher.' The Indians played to the absolute peak of their abilities. And Luis, of course, was the bellwether."

Stan Williams puts it more succinctly. "Cleveland finishing third that year was the miracle of the baseball century!"

So now it's 1969 and the Indians break from the gate and fall on their faces, where they remain for the balance of the schedule as every other team passes them by.

It was the perfect climate for antagonisms to thrive in, and both Luis and Alvin Dark had chips on their shoulders. Luis still felt Dark had been insensitive in his remarks to the press, and Alvin still believed Tiant was jeopardizing his career as well as his team by continuing to work with unorthodox deliveries.

From day one, they were on a collision course.

Luis got off to a horrible start, dropping his first seven decisions.

"When I arrived at spring training I had a stiff shoulder. Then a muscle in my back tightened and I couldn't get rid of it. It bothered me all year long."

He was also troubled by adhesions, a common malady experienced by many pitchers each spring. The human body is equipped with an encapsulated fluid that facilitates mobility in the moving joints: shoulder, hip, etc. But sometimes a sharp twist or turn will break that capsule, allowing the fluid to seep out. The result is a scar tissue that grows between the muscle and the bone, greatly reducing elasticity in the joint.

"You take an arm that's usually active all the time and allow it to rest all winter long and you're going to have a problem when you start pitching again," Stan Williams explains. "It used to take me all spring to tear those adhesions loose, and it usually included internal bleeding. I knew what was happening to Luis and why it was happening. He had always pitched winter ball before. The long rest was hurting him now."

As Schneider noted, Tiant fully expected this would happen.

Meanwhile, Luis' friend Lee Maye—who had been traded to Washington—called him aside one day. "How come you've stopped using your motion?" he asked. "When you're using all those moves, you're confusing everyone. But when you stop using them it's easy to pick up your pitches."

That was all Luis had to hear. It simply reaffirmed what he believed all along, so once again he went back to the herky-jerky gyrations that had been his bread and butter, and once again Alvin Dark's temperature began to rise.

"Luis insisted he'd always pitched this way before," Schneider remembers, "but it seemed he was now doing it to a much greater extent. And he was losing, but you've got to remember that the team behind him wasn't playing anywhere near as well as it had in 1968.

"So Dark began criticizing Luis in the papers again. He insisted Tiant's trouble was that he was destroying his concentration by throwing his head around so much."

Indeed, Alvin's theory appeared to have merit in view of Luis' record, which was 0–7 on May 15.

"He hasn't lost his control to the point where he can't throw strikes," Dark explained, "but he's lost it enough so that he can't pinpoint the ball the way he wants to. You've got to keep your eye on the target. You can't throw your head up into the air, then look over at the scoreboard and then pitch a baseball."

Luis would read that analysis and get madder than hell.

"I didn't want to crucify anybody in the papers," he remembers, "but everybody knew we didn't have a good team. We had no hitting, no double-play combination, no defense. I don't care how you pitch; if you have nobody behind you, you're not going to win. That's what happened to me in Cleveland that season. I told myself I had to win every game by a 1–0 score. That meant I had to go out there and fire-fire-fire for nine innings. Nobody can do that."

Near the end of May the manager used Luis in relief in a lost cause against the expansion Seattle team.

"I did a story with Alvin in which he mentioned the possibility of taking Luis out of the rotation," Schneider says.

Another Cleveland writer did a similar piece, only he concluded his story with the observation that Tiant "is the highest-paid relief pitcher in baseball."

"The guy had to avoid Luis for about a week," Schneider laughs. "If Luis had caught up with him I think he'd have strangled him. And he was almost as mad at Dark. Luis can be a real hothead, you know. He pretends he doesn't know much about English, but he knows everything that's written about him."

Following his single appearance in relief, Tiant went on a spree reminiscent of 1968. He won seven of his next eight outings, dropping only a 4–3 decision to Chicago. Included in that streak was a two-hit shutout against California and a 10-strikeout win over New York.

Then he lost 10 of his next 11 decisions. In three of those games the Indians were shut out. In three others they gave him one run.

Finally Dark called him into the office and told him to curtail his motions. Luis objected and angry words were exchanged.

A few weeks later Alvin summoned Luis again, this time to insist that Tiant stop fooling around in the clubhouse and concentrate instead on preparations for the game.

As far as Luis was concerned, this was the final straw.

"You should be thinking more about baseball instead of joking so much," Alvin suggested.

"Look," Tiant warned, "you don't tell me how to live my life. I've been doing these things since I started playing baseball. How come you didn't tell me this last year when I was winning 21 games?"

"Last year was different," Dark replied. "You were winning then. You're not winning now. And maybe the reason is too much kidding."

"That's not the reason, and you know it," Luis argued back. "I'm not winning because we don't have enough ability on this team. You know that better than I do. If you want to win more, then get a better team. It's not my kidding that's making us lose."

"I'm not so sure about that," Dark replied.

"You live your life and I'll live mine," Luis said. "And when you don't think I'm good enough for this team, or good enough to play for you, then trade me. I don't care."

Dark started to speak, but Luis continued.

"I respect you as my manager, but you're still just a man. And if you're wrong and I'm right, I'm not afraid to tell you. So I'm telling you you don't treat me right. Last year you spoke about me in the papers. This year you did it again. And now you say I've got to be more serious. You never said that last year. You were laughing with everybody else last year. I'll tell you something. I think about games the whole night before I come here. That's enough. The three hours we have before the game I don't want to keep thinking about it. I'll think about it again when I get out there. But all that thinking isn't what makes you a good pitcher. Good teams help make you a good pitcher."

In the middle of July, while the Tribe was stumbling along, a major unheaval was under way in the Cleveland front office. Banner headlines in the local papers told of a rift between Gabe Paul and Alvin Dark.

Paul had once headed a group that owned the team, then he presided over the sale of the franchise to Vern Stouffer, who promptly awarded him a 10-year contract as general manager. It was Paul who hired Dark in 1968, and the two men apparently shared a good friendship.

"Vernon always wanted to be involved and to have people listen to him," Schneider explains, "but he really didn't know shit from shinola when it came to baseball. Gabe really ran the team. Well, Alvin saw what could be done with a situation like that, and he was a pretty ambitious guy. It got kind of messy, but it ended up with Alvin wresting the power from Gabe. We were in New York for a series there on the Fourth of July when I got a call from my office, telling me someone had written that Gabe, for all intents and purposes, had been fired and that Alvin was taking over as GM without the title."

Then Schneider added an afterthought: "It was a disaster!"

For Luis the shift in power had special ramifications. He had been very close to Paul; indeed, Tiant and Harper often visited Gabe's office just to relax and joke with him in 1968.

But there was no such thing as relaxing and joking in Alvin's office, at least not for Luis.

On the contrary, the less he saw of his new boss, the better Luis liked it.

When the season mercifully ended, Tiant's record was 9–20, almost an exact reversal of his 1968 statistic.

He couldn't wait to say goodbye and get on back to Mexico City.

CHAPTER 12

The Trade

Determined he would not endure another springtime like the last one, Luis resumed playing winter ball, this time selecting a team in Hermosillo, a little Mexican border town, which enabled him to be closer to Maria and the kids. Once or twice a month Luis would take the 70-minute trip north to Nogales, an Arizona outpost where an old friend from his Mexican League days ran a little general store. The visits were just a diversion from his Hermosillo routine, but he looked forward to those reunions and to the inevitable bull sessions that conjured up so many happy memories.

When he walked into the store on Friday morning, December 12, however, he sensed something was troubling Natas Garcia, the old second baseman of the Mexico City Reds, as he moved out from behind the counter to extend a welcome.

"What's the matter?" Luis asked.

"You don't know?" Garcia replied.

"Know what?" Luis repeated.

"Cleveland just traded you to Minnesota."

Tiant didn't say a word. He just studied his friend as he tried to collect his thoughts. *Traded?* No one had told him a thing about it; not a phone call, not a visit, not even a note or a telegram.

"Are you sure?" he finally asked.

"Here," Garcia said, offering the morning paper. "Read it."

And so it was. The Indians, the only team he had ever worked for since the day Monchy de Arcos handed Carlos Gonzalez a check for $35,000, thereby procuring his rights from the Mexico City Tigers; the team he had laughed with, and lived with, and suffered with; the team that had been an integral part of his life for the past nine years, from Charleston to Burlington to Portland to Cleveland . . . it had just washed its hands of him without so much as a goodbye, good luck, or *vaya con Dios*.

And for a moment he was hurt—but just for a moment.

"I couldn't believe it," he remembers. "It seemed like a shock. But then I started to feel happy. I knew it was the best thing for me. Besides, I knew down deep inside that it was going to happen. In fact, when I left Cleveland that September I told [pitching coach] Jack Sanford, 'I won't be back.' I was sure Dark was going to get rid of me."

So was Russ Schneider. "Alvin had assumed all of the power, and he just did not like the way Luis was pitching. He felt he was over the hill anyway."

Nor was Gabe Paul surprised, even though it was a move he probably never would have considered had he remained the man who pulled the strings. "It was a foregone conclusion," Gabe says. "Alvin didn't like him and that's all there was to it. But don't ask me why. I don't know the answer. Alvin wasn't confiding in me at that time."

The trade didn't perplex Luis as much as the series of showdowns that led up to it.

"Sports are funny," he theorizes. "When you're winning it makes no difference if you're fat or skinny, if you're funny or quiet, if you do things in a certain way or not. But once you lose, no matter what the reason is, everybody starts looking for an explanation. And I think that's stupid. When I won 21 games in 1968 I don't think I ever weighed less than 205 pounds. I never got tired, and I went nine innings most of the time. But in 1965 when I was 11–11 everyone told me to go home and lose weight. And when that didn't make any difference, they began to complain about the way I threw. Then Alvin even got mad at me for laughing too much. But I did all of these things in 1968 and I didn't hear anybody saying I was a bad pitcher then."

Ah, *¡carajo!* Maybe things would be different in Minnesota.

The transaction involved six players: four Twins in exchange for Luis and his pal Stan Williams.

When first informed of the news, Stan kidded reporters: "If Luis's not going, I'm not going!" But he knew Tiant would be happy to escape the Cleveland morass, and personally he was delighted to be accompanying Luis out the back door.

Minnesota paid a high price for Tiant (9–20) and Williams (6–14):

• Dean Chance, the onetime Bo Belinsky running mate who won 20 games for the 1964 Angels, had come to the Twins in 1967 and won 20 more during that memorable down-to-the-wire race with Boston and Detroit; in 1968 he had been 16–16; but in 1969 a troublesome shoulder resulted in a paltry 5–4 record. At the age of 28, he was still a valuable property;

• Ted Uhlaender, a fleet left-handed-hitting outfielder, was a personal favorite of Alvin Dark's, and it was no secret the Cleveland manager wanted him with the Tribe. When Uhlaender fell into disfavor with Twins' president Calvin Griffith, his departure was assured. Ted was 29;

• Bob Miller was a journeyman right-handed pitcher whose 5–5 record with the Twins in 1969 was his best since going 7–7 with the Dodgers in 1964. He was regarded as a thrown-in;

• Perhaps the key figure, as far as the Indians were concerned, was young Graig Nettles, whom many people believed was destined for stardom, both at the plate and at third base. Graig was 25.

Reactions varied, but the general consensus seemed to be that the Indians got the better of the swap.

"The Indians, of course, are gambling that Dean Chance will come back, and they apparently doubt that Tiant will," sports editor Hal Lebovitz suggested in the Cleveland *Plain Dealer*. "I think Luis is a better bet to make it. If the performances of Chance and

Tiant cancel each other out, it becomes a brilliant deal for the Indians."

"For a long time that trade looked terribly one-sided in our favor," Russ Schneider remembers. "There was no great lament over letting Tiant get away."

Indeed, the lamentations were all in Minnesota.

"The deal got a lot of bad reaction in our local press," says Twins publicity director Tom Mee. "Everyone felt we were giving up too much, especially in Nettles. The general feeling was that Chance, Miller and Uhlaender should have been enough. We were really second-guessed."

As he returned home to Mexico City for the holidays, Luis had not only made the mental adjustment, but also had actually begun feeling an impatience as the days and weeks of winter slipped by.

The Twins had finished first in the American League West in 1969, scoring more runs than anybody else in the league and batting for a higher aggregate average than all of their peers as well. Rod Carew won the batting championship (.332), Harmon Killebrew captured the home run (49) and RBI (140) titles, and Tony Oliva topped the league in hits (197) and doubles (39).

With that kind of a supporting cast behind him, *anything* was possible. March just couldn't come fast enough.

CHAPTER 13

Fractured Hopes

After nine seasons of managing the Angels, following an earlier six-year hitch as boss of the Giants, Bill Rigney was just beginning his new regime with the Twins when Luis arrived at training camp in Orlando in the spring of 1970.

But the Cricket, as some folks called him, needed no introduction to Tiant. Bill had been in the opposing dugout when Luis, making the fifth start of his rookie season, blanked the Angels on four hits. On other occasions he had seen Luis throw two-hitters, three-hitters and four-hitters at his ball club; one night he sat spellbound as Luis fanned 16 Angels while nailing down a 3–2 decision.

Now it was time to watch his brethren squirm a bit.

"As soon as I saw him start doing that hesitation stuff, I smiled," Rigney remembers. "I knew there'd be all kinds of bitching and moaning in the other dugouts, and I thought that was just great."

And the Twins thought Luis was kind of great, too.

"I'll never forget the first time I saw him walk into the showers with a cigar in his mouth," publicist Tom Mee laughs. "The whole team cracked up. We thought he forgot it was there. Then we

found out he *always* smokes while taking a shower! He became
our clubhouse comedian right away. But his value to the team
went much farther than that. Luis was great for team spirit. If he
saw a kid getting out of line, or maybe just straying a bit, he'd
quietly talk with him. Players began coming to him looking for
opinions, and Luis would always tell them what he thought—not
just what he felt they wanted to hear. And they always listened because it was obvious this guy's head was screwed on right."

Mee had his own reasons for rejoicing in Tiant's arrival.

"I liked him," Tom says. "He was always ready and willing to
help me when I needed someone for an appearance. You know, a
lot of ballplayers will tell you they'll go somewhere and then just
never show up. But you could rely on Luis. If he promised you
he'd attend some function, he was there when the time came. I
thought he was a heck of a guy."

But the thing Luis wanted to do most—pitch, the way he knew
he could pitch—eluded him almost from day one. Oh, he was taking a regular turn throughout the exhibition schedule, and getting
the ball across more often than not, but it wasn't moving the way
he wanted it to, mainly because *he* wasn't moving the way he
wanted to.

There was a persistent stiffness in his shoulder, much like the
discomfort he felt the previous spring in Arizona. "I knew I
wasn't pitching the way I could, but I kept getting guys out and
winning, and that's all that seemed to matter," he recalls.

When the season got under way, both the Twins and Luis were
off and flying. Minnesota, the defending American League West
champion, seized an early lead and quickly established itself as the
team to beat once again. And Luis rode the crest of that wave,
reeling off five early victories in a row.

But the shoulder continued to bother him.

"Don't worry about it," trainer George Lentz counseled.
"You've got a tight muscle back there. That's all. One of these
days you're going to feel it pop back into place and it won't bother
you any more."

Luis faced Milwaukee (formerly Seattle) in his sixth start, and
the game was nothing less than all of his winter's dreams coming
true. Every man in the Minnesota lineup contributed to an

awesome 16-hit assault, but none more so than Luis himself as he hit three singles, drove in three runs, and scored a couple more. Minnesota eventually prevailed by an 11–2 count, hiking its first-place record to 29–12, while Tiant's record increased to a league-leading 6–0.

It was never like this in Cleveland.

Still, something wasn't right.

"He wasn't throwing hard," according to his pal, Tommy Harper, the Milwaukee third baseman. "He still gave it the big windup, but the ball wasn't coming in as fast as it used to. He began throwing a lot of breaking stuff. I remember going back to our bench and telling Don Mincher that Tiant didn't seem to have his usual heat. He wasn't throwing like the Luis I knew."

After yielding a two-out homer to Harper in the seventh, Tiant tried to smoke one past Mike Hegan. *Pop!* He felt a sharp, sudden twinge in his shoulder.

"But it didn't bother me," he remembers, "because I kept thinking about what the trainer told me. I just told myself the muscle was stretching back to where it was supposed to be."

Hegan walked, then Luis struck out Danny Walton to retire the side and headed back to the dugout.

He was sure his troubles were over.

He had no idea they were just beginning.

As he warmed up to begin the eighth inning the pain in his shoulder intensified. Luis turned toward the Minnesota dugout, signaled for pitching coach Merv Grissom, and then took himself out of the game.

"I feel okay now," he assured writers later in the training room, even kidding with them about his .434 batting average. ("Maybe they'll have to make me an outfielder.") He even made it a point to emphasize how content he was in his new surroundings. "I go out there confident now," he smiled. "I know these guys will score for me. I don't have to worry about one run tying the game and two runs beating me."

Anyone peering through the cloud of cigar smoke would have easily assumed Tiant was the happiest man in the major leagues.

But three days later, when he tried to work out on the sidelines, Luis discovered he couldn't throw a baseball more than 10 feet!

He summoned the pitching coach, who summoned the doctor, who ordered him sent to a specialist for an examination.

"I didn't panic," Luis remembers, "but I was starting to worry."

Dr. Harvey O'Phelan was a prominent orthopedic surgeon who, in addition to looking after University of Minnesota athletes and serving the 1972 U. S. Olympic Team in Munich, also administered to the needs of the Minnesota Twins.

On Monday morning, June 1, as the Twins flew east toward Yankee Stadium, Luis and teammate Tony Oliva, also bothered by a shoulder ailment, made their way downtown to the Metropolitan Medical Building at the corner of Eighth and Chicago in Minneapolis.

Dr. O'Phelan took X-ray shots of Tiant's right shoulder, then excused himself and went into an adjacent room to view the negatives.

Tony and Luis kidded for a while, but then Tiant's eye caught Dr. O'Phelan as the doctor held the negatives up to a light for closer inspection.

"Look," Luis whispered to Oliva, "something's wrong."

Tony turned to watch the doctor.

"Why's he shaking his head like that?" Luis wondered.

"It's nothing," Oliva replied.

"Something's wrong," Luis insisted. "He's looking funny."

"It's nothing," Tony assured him. "Wait and see."

A few minutes later Dr. O'Phelan returned.

"Luis," he said, "come with me. I want to show you something."

Tiant got up off the table, grabbed his shirt and hurried into the next room.

"See this line here?" Dr. O'Phelan asked, pointing out a pencil-like image on the picture.

"What is it?" Luis wanted to know.

"That's a crack in your bone," the doctor replied.

The injury was officially diagnosed as a fractured scapula, which is the wing bone in the back portion of the shoulder.

It's often the result of a sudden, extreme effort to hurl or throw

an object. Javelin throwers, for instance, are particularly suscep-
tible to this type of injury. But not baseball pitchers.

"I had never seen it in a baseball player before," Dr. O'Phelan
says. "It's a very unusual type of injury."

There was only one immediate remedy he could suggest. Rest.

So the Twins placed Tiant on the 21-day disabled list and called
up 19-year-old rookie Bert Blyleven from their Evansville farm
club.

Despite Dr. O'Phelan's insistence that Tiant's injury was just
temporary, the prophets of doom began to surface, in the media,
in the grandstands and all around the league.

"Everybody thought I was through," Luis remembers, "but the
doctor kept giving me confidence."

And it wasn't just false hope to ease the patient, even though
Dr. O'Phelan had no way of knowing how long the healing process would take.

"As far as I could tell," he says, "the fragments were not dis-
placed, so the fracture, per se, should have healed with no problem. But what other damage he might have done to the shoulder,
such as in the area involving the soft tissues, was indeterminate
at that time. I was confident he could come back from the injury,
but I didn't know how long it would take. The only way we
could treat the fracture was to put the extremity at rest."

A month slipped by, during which time the Twins continued to
pull away from their nearest divisional rivals, the Athletics and
the Angels.

The doctor gave Luis the green light to begin throwing again,
but warned him to stop at the first hint of pain.

"I couldn't get what had happened out of my mind," Luis says.
"Each time I got ready to throw I kept thinking it would happen
again."

He remained on the sidelines for another month. Little by little
the stiffness in his shoulder abated, but the apprehension in his
mind continued to grow.

On Monday, August 3, Luis was reactivated, but, as Harper
had observed back in May, he wasn't the same Tiant whose pirouettes and *heat* made him one of baseball's premier pitchers just
two short seasons ago.

In four decisions down the homestretch Tiant's record was 1–3, giving him an overall record of 7–3 for 1970.

Minnesota easily repeated as Western Division champion, beating out Oakland by nine games, but then was clobbered by Baltimore in the league playoffs, three games to none. Luis pitched just two thirds of an inning in those playoffs, a dramatic contrast to those happy weeks in May when he owned the finest record in the majors.

"But let me tell you something about this guy," Rigney smiled, "because I think it says a lot about what Luis means to team spirit. We clinched our division in a game out at Oakland. Don't forget now, Luis hadn't pitched in quite a while. But I can still see him parading around the clubhouse with his cigar and a bottle of champagne, leading the celebration. In fact, I've got a picture at home that shows the team that night, and the happiest face in the group belonged to Luis. It only proves how much winning means to this man."

CHAPTER 14

The End of the Line?

Questions, like an endless series of storm clouds, hovered over Tiant's head all winter long as he waited for spring training, 1971, and what he hoped would be a new and fresh beginning. Even when he was riding high with that 6–0 record the previous May and his team was staking an early claim on the divisional title, Luis hadn't known a full measure of joy. The persistent shoulder pains had been a constant mental burden until, at last, all of his worst fears were realized when Dr. O'Phelan announced his findings.

Perhaps if he had come back with just a small flourish, if he had made a modest contribution down the stretch run, there would have been ample reason to believe he was well along the road to recovery and the winter months would have been viewed as money in the bank, in terms of convalescence.

Instead, they simply harbored his apprehensions. Even for an incurable optimist like Luis, the facts offered no trace of hope. He had finished the 1970 campaign on a down note, leaving him 5½ months to ponder his future. They might have been the longest months of his life, especially since continued rest was mandatory.

No winter ball simply meant a lot more time to sit and think and worry.

When spring training convened, Luis started throwing with intensity. There was a monkey on his back, and the only way he was going to shake it off was by bulling his way back into the starting rotation. He threw and ran and worked out with the fervor of a rookie, for, indeed, even after seven seasons in the big time, he had no more tenure than a young stud fresh off the farm.

Rigney gave him his first test when the Twins traveled a few miles south to Winter Haven for an exhibition match with the Red Sox. Tiant threw hard, but his control was terrible and then, midway through the game, the roof fell in completely when he pulled a muscle in his rib cage, a fluke mishap that would cost him more than two weeks on the sidelines.

As he left the contest the general consensus up in the press box was that Tiant had reached the end of the line.

"It was kind of sad," Boston publicist Bill Crowley recalls. "Here was a guy who had always looked so good when he pitched against us for Cleveland, and now a group of us were sitting up there and agreeing that he just didn't have it any more. It appeared that he had nothing left."

The word spread quickly along the baseball grapevine. Tommy Harper, working out at the Brewers' camp in Sun City, Arizona, couldn't believe the latest scuttlebutt. "The feeling seemed to be that Luis was all washed up. That's what people were saying."

Perhaps they were, but Luis wasn't listening.

"I never gave up," he says today, looking back. "I kept telling myself as long as I could get the ball up to home plate I was going to stay in baseball. And that had nothing to do with money. It was just love of the game. You've heard of people who say baseball is all they know? Well, that's me, too. I'm like that. I've loved it all my life. So did my father and so did my uncles. Everyone back in Cuba loved the game. So I didn't let the things people were saying bother me, and I never thought of quitting."

Though the injury prohibited him from throwing, Luis put his days to good use by running and exercising. When his arm was ready, he wanted to be damned sure the rest of his body was, too.

"I watched him," Rigney remembers. "All the time he was unable to pitch he kept working out at his own pace, and I really admired that. The pace never varied; it was always good and solid. He'd run miles every day. No one ever had to push him."

Luis appeared in one more game before training camp ended, against Atlanta, and thought he did a credible job. So did his friend Orlando Cepeda, the Braves' first baseman. "You're looking good again," he assured him, after Tiant picked up credit for his first win.

But that's not what the record said. In the entire training period Luis had worked just eight innings. His ERA was a fat 7.88, and he had allowed 14 hits.

There was nothing to do now but cross his fingers and hope the Twins would look behind those figures to where the real story laid.

The Park Plaza Hotel was a veritable beehive on Wednesday, March 31, as members of the Minnesota entourage—players, coaches, writers, front-office personnel, equipment managers, et al.—gathered their belongings and prepared to break camp the following morning.

Six days later a capacity crowd and a standing ovation were expected to greet the squad as it ran onto the infield at Memorial Stadium for the traditional introductions prior to the season's opener against the Brewers.

There was an excitement in the air, a great sense of expectation, and old-timers will assure you it's that way every year, for every team, regardless of rank, on the eve of breaking camp.

But Howie Fox, the club's traveling secretary and—as a result —the man responsible for arranging travel accommodations, didn't share the mood of frivolity, for he had just been told to carry out a most unpleasant duty.

Luis stopped packing his bags and reached for the ringing phone in his room.

"Luis," Fox asked, "would you come down to see me, please?"

The Twins had decided to drop Tiant. Completely. No assignment to the minors where he might work his way back; no disabled lists which might give him more healing time; not even a trade to some other club which might have found a spot for him. Plain and simple, they just decided to wash their hands of him. Winners of the American League West crown two years in a row, and now expected to get off to another flying start, they didn't feel they had any room for a sore-armed veteran, especially one who had been 9–20 two years earlier, 1–3 over the major portion of the previous season and, most recently, a bomb in spring training.

In a business that relies so heavily on "the book," on percentages, on sure things, keeping Tiant was a luxury the Twins felt they could no longer afford.

"I don't think it was a mistake at the time," Dr. O'Phelan says. "The team had to cut its squad down to 25 players, and Luis hadn't done anything all spring. He could hardly lift his arm, even though the fracture had healed. The question was, how long could the Twins wait? Mr. [Calvin] Griffith asked me how long it would be before Luis was completely healthy again. One year? Two years? I had to tell him I didn't know if he'd ever come back. At the time we had no indications."

Tom Mee explains the situation in stronger terms. "Luis was let go because he appeared to be all washed up. Everyone agreed it was a proper decision."

Well, not exactly everyone.

"I thought what was happening was a tragedy," Stan Williams recalls. "So did most of the ballplayers. I knew Luis when he was sound, when he was one of the top pitchers in all of baseball, and I was so sure in my heart that he was not finished. I knew about the physical problems he'd been having. I felt once he got over them, he'd be back on the upswing."

But baseball, as previously pointed out, is a business. The simple game that Luis loved as a boy in Cuba had evolved into a multimillion-dollar corporate giant in America, and corporate giants have never been known to look beyond the bottom line.

In Tiant's case, the bottom line read *finished*.

"I'm sorry to tell you this, Luis," Howie Fox began, "but I've got to give you your unconditional release. But wherever you go from here, I hope you win 20 games."

Luis was stunned and hurt.

"Don't give me that baloney," he blurted. "If you think I can still win 20 games, why don't you keep me here?"

Fox shrugged helplessly.

"Give me the release and let me get out of here," Luis demanded. "I don't want any more advice or good wishes."

Then he sought out Griffith, the team's president and general manager, with whom he had agreed to take a $10,000 pay cut following his injury-riddled 1970 season. Luis wanted to know why the Twins wouldn't at least give him an opportunity to iron out his problems in the minors.

"He didn't say anything to me," Tiant recalls with a hint of bitterness, "but then he told reporters he could get four or five young kids for the money he was giving me."

The verdict, he then realized, was irreversible.

Later that afternoon Luis returned to his room and placed a call to Mexico City. Under other circumstances he probably wouldn't have taken his troubles to Maria—that wasn't his way of handling adversity—but she was expecting him to be in Minnesota if she had to reach him, so now he had to call to explain why he wouldn't be flying there in the morning.

Maria, meanwhile, had been having her own problems to contend with on the home front. Both of the children were ill, and she, ironically, was bothered by a soreness in her arm. Her husband's call was like an elixir, or so she thought until she sensed the anxiety in his voice.

As Luis carefully explained the situation to her, purposely avoiding any suggestion of alarm, Maria began to cry.

"What are you doing that for?" he kidded.

She continued to weep.

"Don't cry," Luis pleaded. "This is nothing. I'll look for another team. I'll find work. Just don't worry."

"I'll look for a job," she finally said.

"What?" he laughed. "Are you crazy?"

"But what about the children?"

"It's going to be all right, you'll see. Please don't worry."

She agreed, and then they talked about the kids for a while, and about the neighborhood news, and, at last, they said goodbye.

Luis placed the receiver back into its cradle and flopped down on the bed, right beside the partially packed suitcase.

And then he cried, too.

The next morning was getaway day. Scores of garment bags and leather cases and banged-up footlockers were scattered around the lobby of the Park Plaza as the Twins waited for the caravan of trucks and cars that would take them on the first leg of their long journey north.

There was the usual amount of kibitzing and horsing around, along with the inevitable confusion of moving a major league baseball team from one town to another.

And there was also a sense of awkwardness in the air, for Luis was right in the midst of the group, laughing and kidding as always, even though everyone was painfully aware that he was really no longer a member of the family.

Rigney called him aside. "I don't know," he told him, "maybe they're doing you a favor. But I'd like to say one thing. You've done everything I asked you to do for us, even when you were hurt—maybe even some things you shouldn't have tried to do, because you weren't capable. But perhaps this will turn out to be a blessing if this thing—whatever's wrong with you—goes away. But that's not what I wanted to say. Look, if there's anything you think I can do to help you, in any direction, like calling another club for you or something, I just want you to know I'd be happy to do it."

It wasn't an empty gesture.

"No, it wasn't," Rigney says today. "Frankly, I don't think the door should have been closed on him, but there was nothing I could do about it. The people upstairs had made up their minds on him. It was cut and dried. But I wanted to help him if I could. He was such a decent guy, a great man to have on your club, and one helluva competitor when he could pitch. I remember feeling that I was missing a lot. I had seen some of his personality in the time he was with us, but I had never seen the *real* Luis Tiant on the mound."

Rigney's private conference signaled the start of a single-file parade as, one by one, the Twins walked over to shake his hand and bid him farewell.

"It was the most forlorn experience I've ever had in baseball," Tom Mee says. "Luis was practically in tears as we left him there in the lobby."

The dreams of a lifetime—indeed, the dreams of *two* lifetimes, for the father's aspirations were vicariously entwined with the son's—laid shattered at his feet as Luis waved a last goodbye at the caravan that was leaving him behind.

The scene continued to unsettle Tom Mee as he sat back in his seat, waiting for the plane to touch down in Minneapolis. He couldn't seem to shake away the sight of Luis standing all alone. It was more than just a sentimental reaction, however.

"I don't think Luis ever stopped believing he could come back, not even for a moment," Mee explains. "He was sure he could still pitch, but he was afraid he'd never get an opportunity to prove it to anyone else. That's why he was just about in tears when we left him."

PART IV
A New Beginning

CHAPTER 15

The Road to Boston

For the average American workingman the end of a career is a bittersweet crossroad of life. It reaffirms the rapid passage of the years and reminds him—as if he needed any reminder—that the sunset of his days has now begun. And yet, if he's planned wisely, and if he's developed avocations over the years, it begins a long-awaited period of rest and relaxation, of leisurely pursuit of the things that make him happy.

But the professional athlete is not your average American workingman. Even if he's been a superstar, and even if he's financially secure for life, the specter of retirement is often looked upon with horror.

"All of a sudden it hits you," Harvard basketball coach Tom Sanders once explained, a few months before he ended his 13-year career with the Boston Celtics. "You realize the sweetest part of your life is over, and the world is out there waiting like a dragon. Maybe that sounds dramatic, but that's how it is when you're an athlete. When a man stops playing, it's like his whole world is gone."

But Sanders was one of the lucky ones. He had, as the Scriptures admonish, built his house upon a rock. When his time came, he was ready to make a graceful transition to the *real* world. Yet he left with regrets.

Some never look that far ahead, however, and for them the trauma magnifies to monumental proportions.

There's a grand piece of sports folklore in Boston concerning the day two Red Sox players named Gene Conley and Pumpsie Green walked off the team bus in a downtown New York traffic jam and decided to catch a flight to Israel. The story's always good for a belly laugh in the neighborhood pub, mainly because very few people happen to know the *real* story, which isn't funny at all.

Conley was a marvelous six-foot, eight-inch athlete, good enough to have pitched 11 seasons in the major leagues (appearing in three All-Star games and the 1957 World Series) while also playing six seasons in the National Basketball Association (including three with Bill Russell's world champion Celtics).

But now it was late June of 1961 and all the years of heavy drinking and hard playing were at last catching up with him. His body was ravaged, and his once-mighty right arm was loaded up with cortisone. It was getting near All-Star Game time, however, and Gene wanted so much to go out with one Last Hurrah. The Red Sox were playing the Yankees, and New York manager Ralph Houk, who'd be picking the All-Star pitchers, would be watching, he reminded himself. Gene never got more emotionally psyched for a game in his life. But rookie outfielder Carl Yastrzemski dropped a couple of fly balls, and fellow rookie Chuck Schilling booted a sure double play at second, and Conley found himself being lifted out of the game, which the Red Sox eventually lost.

Conley agonized over his misfortune, and later, with the bus mired in Manhattan's commuter congestion, his spirit broke completely.

"C'mon," he said to Pumpsie, his friend, "let's go."

With that, the pair took off and headed to the nearest bar, where Conley proceeded to brood.

"The pressure really got to me that day," says Gene, who's now a very sober, very successful businessman, quite active in his church life and his family life as well. "I always thought I was good enough to keep on playing until I was 40, 45 years old. I never worried about the future. It always seemed so far away. But time sneaked up on me. I couldn't throw any more without pain, and I didn't have a cent put away for the future, or even a job to go to, for that matter. And I just sat in that bus telling myself, *'Hey, Gene, you've got nothing left!'*

"Well, I knew there was a four-day break coming right up—I wasn't *that* stupid—so I grabbed Pumpsie and we just took off. We had nothing special in mind. We started boozing and for two or three days I guess we hit every bar in New York. But that wasn't making me feel any better. All I kept thinking was, *'I'm tired, my arm hurts, I'm getting all this cortisone, I'm near the end of the line, and I've got no money saved.'* It was like the world was closing in on me. And I decided there was only one answer left, and that was the good Lord. So I said, *'Come on, Pumpsie, we're going to Jerusalem to get this squared away!'*

"And that's how it all started. I just felt desperate."

Whether the world was closing in on Luis like it did on Conley, or waiting out there like a dragon, the way Sanders envisioned it, one thing was for very certain: Luis had come to the end of the road as far as the baseball population was concerned, and with opening-day festivities just around the corner at every stop on both big league circuits, he was almost forgotten already.

Future plans? Five minutes before he got that call from Howie Fox, the question would have been laughable. Baseball. What else? Indeed, what else was there? Up to that point in Luis' life there had been nothing else at all. You might as well tell a fish to leave the water, or a bird to leave the sky.

If anyone ever needed a friend, it was Luis Tiant at that hour.

And he had one in Stan Williams.

"Stan helped Luis in so many ways," Tommy Harper says. "When I found out the things he did I was really moved. Stan is one hell of a guy."

How a tall, handsome white dude, born in the parochial little village of Enfield, New Hampshire, and a black, broken-English exile from the tortured land of Cuba ever struck up such a deep, abiding friendship is at once one of the beauties and the mysteries of sports. It's what brought Jack Twyman to Maurice Stokes in his hour of need, and what led Gale Sayers to Brian Piccolo's side in those final hours.

"Luis is the best friend I've ever had in baseball," Stan explains. "I respected him as an athlete, admired his desire and professional attitude and loved him as a person. I guess it was his humor that first attracted me toward him. He's one of the funniest guys I've ever met in my life. But the more I got to know him, the more I discovered what a warm, sensitive, intelligent person he is. I found out the sun rises and sets on Maria and those kids, and I found out how much this game means to him personally, which has nothing to do with cheers and headlines."

And that's why Williams—next to Tiant—was the most horrified man in Orlando when Luis was handed his walking papers.

"This guy is a very dear friend of mine," Stan points out, "but the game of baseball is a dear friend of mine, too, and I knew the game would be cheating itself if it ever allowed Luis to slip away."

All of which is very noble, not to mention rather poetic, but what could Stan Williams do to change the apparent course of history?

Williams had the room adjoining Tiant's, and within hours of the fateful decision it took on the appearance of Mission Control as Stan—assisted by Ron Perranoski—began calling his contacts as quickly as they came to mind.

"Luis' English isn't what you'd call limited," he explains, "but sometimes it might be hard to understand over the phone, especially for a stranger. Besides, I thought it would be easier for a third person to explain the situation than to have Luis put in the position of having to sell himself. And it was going to take some explaining. The last day of spring training is the worst possible time to be cut. Everyone's roster is filled by then, and people are going to be very leery about dropping someone who's made their team in favor of someone who couldn't make another."

Stan's first call was to the Boston organization, primarily because the Red Sox have long enjoyed the reputation of being baseball's most doting employers. Players there were treated first-class. That was common knowledge. "It's sort of a family-type atmosphere up there," Williams explained to Luis. "That's where you want to be."

He left word with a switchboard operator to have either general manager Dick O'Connell or player personnel director Haywood Sullivan return his call, but the message got lost in the shuffle and neither man ever received it.

Perranoski, meanwhile, had placed a call to his friend Billy Martin, the new Detroit manager, urging him to give Luis a shot with the Tigers. But Martin's bullpen was full.

With messages now scattered among switchboards all around the country, Williams finally tracked down an old friend named Ed Roebuck, a former Dodger roommate who was scouting for Atlanta. The Braves, divisional champs in 1969, had fallen 10 games below .500 in 1970, bringing about an ambitious talent hunt. Players were being accepted into the Atlanta farm system on 30-day trial plans. If they showed enough to earn a promotion to the parent club they were immediately offered a contract. If not, they were sent packing again. It was hardly a Welcome Wagon they were running, but at least it was an opportunity.

And that's all Luis wanted.

"This guy can make it," Williams assured Roebuck. "He'll be a feather in your cap. And I'll stake our friendship on that."

Roebuck was clearly impressed. He promised to set the machinery in motion, and, true to his word, a few days later—after Williams, Perranoski and the rest of the Twins had already arrived in Minnesota—he got the green light.

Luis was told to report to Atlanta's affiliate in Richmond, Virginia.

There he would be given 30 days in which to prove that Calvin Griffith had made a terrible mistake.

Pedro Ramos, the old Havana Sugar King star who went on to pitch in the majors for 15 seasons, happened to be in Richmond when Luis arrived.

"If anything was bothering him, he never showed it to me or to anyone else," Ramos recalls. "He believed he could do the job. That was easy to see."

In one of Richmond's first outings manager Clyde King started

Luis against Bradenton, the Pittsburgh representative in the International League. For five innings Tiant's fastball was smoking. Even at the Triple-A level, just one step down from the Bigs, the Bradenton kids had never seen heat like that.

"Why did those people ever let you go?" King asked.

Luis just smiled back. "That's a good question."

A Pirates scout walked over.

"What was wrong with your arm?" he wanted to know.

"Nothing," Luis replied. "I hurt it last year, but it's okay now. But my rib cage bothered me. Now that's okay, too. All I need is work."

"They must have been crazy letting you go," the Pittsburgh man exclaimed.

Luis nodded and gave a shrug. He didn't feel that the comment called for a response.

Had Tiant believed in omens and such, he might have begun wondering what the gods were trying to tell him, for the weather soon raised havoc with Richmond's schedule, causing postponements, cancellations and assorted delays, none of which helped his cause a single bit. Instead of getting steady work, Luis found himself idle for days on end.

But he did make two appearances against the Louisville Colonels, Boston's entry in the league, and Louisville manager Darrell Johnson began to take notice, not so much because of what he saw, but rather because of what he kept hearing.

José Santiago, who had been one of the central figures in Boston's 1967 pennant epic, was pitching for the Colonels, trying to work his way back from an injury. Ramos, one of his good friends, pulled him aside one day and told what was happening to Tiant.

"Even though Luis is a friend of mine," Pedro says, "I am honest to baseball. If I didn't believe he was going to be all right, I would have kept quiet. But I honestly felt there was nothing wrong with Tiant. And like I told José, when a man throws as well as Luis did, and believes in himself the way Luis did, he deserves at least a chance."

Santiago relayed the information to Johnson and to Lee Stange, who was then the pitching coach in Boston's farm system.

Wedding bells ring in Mexico City, 1961.

Rookie of the Year in the Cuban League, 1960–61.

Little Luis gets some tips from his famous dad, 1968.

Hitching a ride with the 1968 ERA champ.

Winter ball with the Caracas Lions, December 1970.

uis and Tommy Harper: "We're better
an brothers."

En route to an early shower.

Darrell Johnson decides to stick w
Luis.

Prior to father-son game at Fenway in 1974.

ollowing famous footsteps: little Luis in
Iilton Little League.

Can you guess who won tonight?

After 15 years, father and son share their first embrace.

Time to go home: Luis escorts
mother and Isabel out of Logan International Airport following emotional reunion; young Luis and Maria flank Señor
Tiant in background.

Señor Tiant prepares for Fenway Park debut.

Just like old times: *bringing heat* across the plate.

Catcher Tim Blackwell offers congratulations.

Señora Tiant joins fans in standing ovation for her son.

Carlton Fisk embraces Luis after dramatic 2–0 shutout over Baltimore in September 1975.

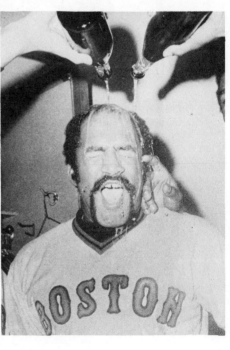

Luis gets traditional shower after Sox clinched 1975 playoffs in Oakland.

Luis gives Yastrzemski a champagne dousing as Red Sox celebrate 1975 American League pennant.

Happy homecoming: Señor Tiant, Jorgito Raspal, young Luis, Luis and Maria (left to right) returning from victorious playoff visit to Oakland.

The final motion of a splendid 6–0 victory in the World Series opener.

Yastrzemski and Tiant in an impromptu dance following win over Reds in Series opener.

Adventure on the basepaths: Luis scoots into second after Evans' sacrifice bunt is thrown wildly to center field; he scores game's first (and winning) run moments later as Yaz singles into right.

A

B

C

D

E

(sequence of photos—A, B, C, D, E
This variety of poses illustrates wh
American League batters are up again
when they face Luis. Photo A shows ho
well he hides the ball from view; pho
B shows a sidearm pitch en route, whi
photo C is an overhand delivery in pro
ress. In photos D and E, the follo
through is complete.

The rules prohibited the Red Sox from formally approaching Tiant while he was under the 30-day agreement with Atlanta, but that didn't stop Stange from making a side trip to Richmond for a closer peek.

"I'd like to see you throw," he said.

By this time Tiant's record was 1–3. In 23 innings he had yielded 22 hits, 16 earned runs, 17 walks and had an ERA of 6.26, higher than he had ever been since the day he first put on a Mexico City uniform.

Stange's request, in view of those statistics, seemed reasonable.

But Luis was upset, or perhaps just self-conscious.

"Look," he told Stange, "I don't think I have to prove I can throw. I know my record's not good now, but I've been pitching with 10, 12 days' rest, and there's no way anyone can do a good job like that. Everywhere we've gone there's been rain or cold or snow or something. We've had about 10 games called off and I've lost my timing again. That's the only thing wrong with me."

Stange reported back to Johnson, who then summoned Santiago.

"Find out when his 30 days are up," Darrell said. "Tell him if he's a free agent then, we'd like to talk with him."

The deadline, Santiago learned, was Saturday, May 15, which also happened to be the weekend Richmond was visiting Louisville.

As the final few days of Tiant's agreement began to slip away, Clyde King grew increasingly uneasy. He, too, believed Luis was just a month or two away from putting it all together again, and he tried to persuade the Braves to call him up, if that's what was necessary to keep him in the organization.

Atlanta declined.

"Then I'm going to sign with Louisville," Tiant announced.

At 10 A.M. that Saturday he walked into the Louisville ball park and sat down with Darrell Johnson.

Johnson had already talked with Dick O'Connell that morning, expressing his confidence that Luis—despite his horrid record—was throwing harder all the time and showed signs of making a complete recovery.

"I don't think he had enough time to get over his injury in

Orlando," Darrell told O'Connell. "But we know what he was like in Cleveland, so what have we got to lose?"

"Talk with him," O'Connell advised. "See if he'll sign a contract with your club, and tell him we'll bring him to Boston at the earliest opportunity, based on your recommendation."

"Fine," Johnson replied. "What should I offer him?"

"Find out what he's making now," O'Connell said, "then offer him $1,000 or $1,500 more. If he makes it, it's a good investment."

When Luis arrived he shook hands with Johnson and the two men talked briefly about the Boston situation and where Luis might fit in.

"All I'm looking for is a regular contract," Tiant said. "This 30-day business is no good. It makes too much pressure. I want a regular contract and then some regular work."

Johnson nodded in agreement. "Don't worry about that," he promised, "I'll use you every fourth day."

Then he reached for the phone on his desk and placed a call to Boston.

"Dick," he said, "I've got Luis Tiant sitting here in my office right now and I'd like to offer him a contract."

O'Connell smiled. "Sign him."

As soon as Luis began throwing for the Colonels, Johnson realized a coup was in the making. Though he was nowhere near top form, Tiant was nevertheless working effortlessly. What really caught Darrell's eye, however, was the way the man had comported himself.

"He was such a competitive type of guy," the manager remembers. "I could see it every time he walked out to the mound. He knew what he wanted to do out there and he had the confidence to back it up, even though he was still in the process of regaining his control. I was more than satisfied with what I saw."

Less than three weeks later Darrell picked up his phone again.

"Dick," he said, "without even knowing who your best pitcher is up there right now, or even your second- and third-best, I can tell you this man's going to be better. He's improving every day. If you can do it, considering the paperwork and everything, I recommend that you bring him to Boston and pitch him regularly."

O'Connell then contacted Haywood Sullivan and promptly dispatched him to Rochester, New York, where the Colonels were playing a doubleheader the following night. He wanted a second opinion. O'Connell also wanted him to check on the progress Santiago was making.

Luis worked the opener that night and breezed to a 3–0 victory. Santiago pitched the nightcap and won, 3–1, losing his shutout bid in the final inning.

Haywood dashed to the nearest phone and dialed O'Connell's number.

"Luis is better than three or four guys we've got up there right now," he reported.

"Talk with him," Dick said. "Find out how he feels."

Sullivan returned to the Louisville locker room and sought out Tiant, whose record was now 2–2 with a 2.61 ERA. In 31 innings Luis had fanned 29 and walked 11. *And he was still trying to regain his control!*

"Can you meet me for breakfast in the morning?" Haywood asked.

"Pick a time," Luis grinned.

Bright and early the following day the two men slid into a booth, waved for a pot of coffee and then got down to business.

"Are you ready to come back to the big leagues?" Sullivan asked.

"I didn't sleep all night," Luis confided, "because I thought you were going to ask me this. You're damned right I'm ready."

And so, just 20 days after he joined the Colonels, Tiant was packing his bags again, only this time he was smiling.

Next stop: Fenway Park.

CHAPTER 16

A Melancholy Summer

In the years that followed after Castro's conversion to communism, Luis' life was divided into two main components: his baseball career in the States and his family life in his adopted hometown of Mexico City. Cuba became a memory, a lingering heartache, a part of his past that followed him everywhere he went, even though he rarely discussed it with anyone other than his tightest circle of friends. Though the emotional ties to his homeland remained, all of the physical ties had been severed by the passage of time.

One can well imagine, therefore, his elation in later years when he again crossed paths with three of his boyhood buddies who had also left the island before the exits were boarded up: Juanito Quintana, Jorgito Raspall and Felix Fernandez, all of whom had driven new roots into American soil.

Quintana would be the last of the trio he'd catch up with.

The reunion with Raspall occurred in 1969 when Jorgito, relaxing in his Somerville, Massachusetts, home, turned on his television set one day to catch a Red Sox game. "Olga," he yelled to his wife, "look, it's Tiant! He's playing in Boston!" Jorgito scurried to his phone, called Fenway Park and left a message for Luis. A few hours later the phone rang. "Jorgito!" the familiar voice rang out. "I don't believe it's you." Raspall got into his car, drove into the city to the ball park, embraced his long-lost friend and brought him home to Somerville for a dinner and reunion that lasted into the wee hours of the following morning.

The friendship with Fernandez was also rekindled during Tiant's years in Cleveland. Whenever the Tribe played in Boston, the pair would get together for meals and reminiscence. Luis even called upon Fernandez to open up his apartment to friends like José Tartabull in 1966 and Vicente Romo in 1969, giving them someplace to call home until they got settled following the trades that sent them to the Red Sox.

The day before he left Louisville, Tiant called Felix to tell him he was on the way and to get the extra bed ready! Like Tartabull and Romo before him, Luis was coming to stay for a while.

On June 3 he arrived in Boston, and four days later flew out of Logan International Airport with the Red Sox contingent, bound for a 12-game western road trip.

Manager Eddie Kasko immediately placed him in the starting rotation, which at that time included Jim Lonborg, Ray Culp, Gary Peters and his former teammate on the Indians staff, Sonny Siebert.

"We were looking for help," Eddie explains.

But no one was looking for miracles.

"I think all we really wanted Luis to do was to bridge a gap for us," Haywood Sullivan says. "We were hoping an experienced player might help us plug a hole until some of our good young kids could take over."

Luis made his first appearance on June 11 in Kansas City and bombed. "The latest investment by the Red Sox looked about as sound as taking a bagful of money and throwing it off Pier 4 into the Atlantic," veteran Boston baseball writer Clif Keane reported in the *Globe*. Luis lasted only one inning, giving up three hits, three walks and five runs.

"The ball was all over the place," Kasko recalls. "But yet you could see the velocity was beginning to pick up."

Tiant was given six starts in July, losing four and winning none. Still Kasko stood behind him. He had pitched three-hit ball for seven innings against the Yankees, losing 2–1 on Roy White's two-run homer. Then, in what had to be an emotional appearance against the Twins in Minnesota, Luis hurled shutout ball for 10 innings, striking out nine of his springtime teammates, only to be lifted for a pinch-hitter and thereby deprived of getting credit for Boston's eventual 3–0 victory.

"I threw 154 pitches," he explained to writers, "so I told him [Kasko] he'd better take me out of there before I hurt my arm again. It feels 100 per cent better than it did earlier this year, but I'm still not all the way back."

Indeed, he wasn't. In fact, he appeared to grow weaker in his next five starts, only once lasting more than four innings, so on August 10 Kasko reluctantly ended his great experiment and shipped Tiant off to the bullpen where his critics had loudly insisted he belonged in the first place.

"I remember those days so well," Fernandez says. "It seemed nobody believed Luis was going to make it. I was *hoping* he would, but Luis *knew* he would. He never stopped believing that. He always had faith in himself, and—though he wouldn't show it publicly—he'd get very mad at people who said he was all washed up. He'd come home and tell me they didn't know a thing about baseball."

While Fernandez, a language teacher at nearby Brookline High School, would sit at his table, poring over classroom work, Luis would work out with weights for a while, then sit in a chair and fret.

"I'd look up and see him sitting there, staring out the window deep in thought," Felix confided, "and I'd feel badly for him because I knew the worries that were going through his mind. I'd offer him a drink, but he'd refuse, and then he'd say, 'If only I had thrown some other pitch!' Night after night he'd sit there, playing games over and over in his mind, trying to understand what he was doing wrong."

Fernandez was more than a sympathetic ear; he was also Tiant's baseball guru. On more than one occasion Luis pitched to Felix. "Watch how this one breaks," Luis would say as he wound up and fired.

Inevitably, Felix would come back with the same advice.

"You're not following through the way you used to," he told him. "You're still afraid of that shoulder, aren't you? It's not going to break again. It's the strongest bone in your body now. You've got to let loose. You can't keep holding back. You're losing too much on your pitches."

In late July and early August the Sox went away on a 14-game trip, and when they returned Luis had good news for Felix.

"You know what I found out?" he announced. "My shoulder *is* stronger!"

"Who told you that?" Felix asked.

"A doctor. He told me broken bones get stronger when they heal."

Fernandez didn't tell Tiant, but he was privately relieved to hear the news.

"When I kept telling that to Luis, I didn't really know if it was true or not," he smiles. "It was something I thought I remembered reading. Maybe it was a lie, but it was a *good* lie, I think. And once that doctor told Luis the same thing, it was a turning point for him. I could see he was much more relaxed."

On Saturday, August 14, in his third relief appearance since being demoted from Kasko's rotation, Luis threw seven innings of three-hit ball against Kansas City, striking out 10 and walking two. He also set the stage for Kasko's ejection when, after nodding four times to no one in particular, he whirled and rifled a strike to George Scott at first, apparently catching Kansas City's Bob Oliver off the bag. At least that's the way the outraged Scott saw it, but umpire Marty Springstead didn't concur, and thus Oliver was ruled safe. Kasko's uncharacteristic rage earned him an immediate trip to the showers.

It really made no difference, since Kansas City was already ahead, 6–1, thanks to its early bombardment of starter Gary Peters, which resulted in five first-inning runs.

Tiant's record remained 0–6, and he had to wonder if he'd ever get credit for a win in 1971.

Finally, on August 31, in his eighteenth Red Sox appearance, he again relieved Peters, this time against the rampaging Orioles in Fenway Park. He struck out the first two men he faced to squelch a Baltimore rally in the seventh, then retired the O's in order in the eighth and ninth. When Carl Yastrzemski's single off the wall scored Mike Fiore (who was pinch-hitting for Tiant) in the bottom of the ninth, Luis had his first major league victory in more than a year, 4–3.

And no one was any happier for him than Kasko, the quiet, oft-maligned skipper whose constant reassurance had meant so much to Luis throughout the season.

"You know what made me like that guy so much?" Eddie says. "His professionalism. I know that sounds corny, but it's true. With all of the things that were on his mind that summer, he never showed any signs of discontent, even when I finally had to send him to the bullpen. He never bitched or moaned. The man was a professional in every sense of the word."

But the man was also 1–7 at season's end. In two months he'd reach his thirty-first birthday, and everyone knew Boston had a bumper crop of kids who couldn't be kept down on the farms much longer.

Time was running out for Luis. Again.

"As that season came to an end, it seemed Luis was often becoming melancholy," Felix Fernandez recalls. "One of his greatest concerns in life is being a good provider for his family. Luis is a very traditional family man. He'd often talk about family feeling in a very proverbial manner. It meant a lot to him. He'd tell me: 'Everyone has a family, but mine can't be with me. I have to pitch, I have to make it, so I can bring them up here with me and make a good home together.' He'd think about that, then think about the way his season had been going, and he'd get into one of those melancholy moods again. Luis doesn't let many things bother him, but this was different. And I know he was very worried about what would happen in spring training the next year."

It was an altogether reasonable concern, for Luis didn't have a lot going for himself, other than his friends' best wishes.

"I'm sure he worried a lot that winter," Haywood Sullivan says. "Here was an older ballplayer, who didn't have a particularly good season, and who had already been released twice in one year. When that happens a man is apt to feel stereotyped, as if he must show more than the next guy does just in order to prove that his record is misleading. I imagine that's what was going through Luis' mind at the end of 1971."

But at least he'd have one foot in the door when spring training opened, because Eddie Kasko was determined to give him one more honest shot at a steady job.

"The only problem I could see would be holding off the wolves," Kasko remembers thinking as he headed home that autumn. "I was sure if I could get Luis through the first month of the season, he'd show enough to warrant keeping him on the team. But if the young kids started showing a lot in camp I knew the critics would be all over Luis. And I'm sure he realized that, too."

As he prepared to leave for Mexico City that September, Luis talked with Felix about the future.

"I'll always remember the way he acted that day," Fernandez smiles. "He told me to have the apartment ready again next year. We discussed the possibility of the young players taking away his job and, like I said, sometimes Luis talks in a proverbial way. He gave me a funny look, then said,

> '*Deja a los otros caballos correr primero y levantar polvo yo los alcanzaré.*'

Then we both laughed."

Translation?

> Let the anxious horses run first and make a lot of noise and dust, and I will get them.

CHAPTER 17

Revival in the Bullpen

Luis spent most of the 1971–72 winter in Venezuela playing for the La Guaira Sharks. On November 15, just after the season got under way, he threw a no-hitter at the Caracas Lions. There was no way in the world he wasn't going to be ready when the opening bell sounded at Winter Haven in March.

Tommy Harper didn't have a chance to talk with his pal all winter, but there'd be plenty of time for that when springtime rolled around. On October 10, the Red Sox had stunned the baseball world by pulling off a massive 10-player swap with Milwaukee, sending George Scott, Jim Lonborg, Billy Conigliaro, Ken Brett, Joe Lahoud and Don Pavletich to the Brewers in exchange for Marty Pattin, Lew Krausse, Pat Skrable and Harper.

For the first time since 1968, Tommy and Luis were going to be teammates again.

"When the time came to report," Harper recalls, "I got into my car and drove from Tampa over to Winter Haven. And of course I got lost. I must have driven around that damned lake there a dozen times. I finally got to my room late that night. Camp officially opened the next morning, and it was really kind of an anticipation thing for me, you know? All the way to the park I had this funny feeling, just knowing that Luis knew I was coming. There was no doubt in my mind that he was going to get there early, just to put something in my locker or to set up some kind of joke on me. Just thinking about him doing something like that made me laugh. And sure enough, the moment I walked through the door I could hear that high, squeaky voice, yelling and screaming, telling everyone in the room that *'the ugliest man in the world just joined our team!'* I looked at him, and he looked at me, and we laughed so hard we cried. I just knew it was going to be *that* type of a season with him around again."

For a while it appeared it might be *no* kind of a season as the Players Association staged a wildcat, 13-day walkout, the first general strike in baseball history. The result was the cancellation of 86 regular-season games and a 10-day delay in the start of the schedule. More than that, however, it meant an uneven schedule, since action commenced on a single date with no allowances made for the staggered start built into the original timetable. Consequently, in the American League East three teams (Detroit, Cleveland and Milwaukee) would play 156 games; two (Boston and New York) would play 155; and one (Baltimore) would play 154.

The eventual ramifications of that arrangement would be enormous, especially for the Red Sox.

Despite his jester's greeting for Harper, Luis remained in a pensive mood throughout most of the 1972 spring training. One day, as he dined alone, he was approached by John Alevizos, at the time a vice president of the team.

"Mind if I sit down?" Alevizos asked.

"No," Tiant replied, although his mind immediately flashed back to that 1971 visit with Howie Fox. He instinctively braced for bad news.

"I've been watching you," Alevizos began, "and I know how hard you've been working. Whether you realize it or not, you've been setting one hell of a good example for all of these kids here. I'm sure it hasn't been easy for you. So I'd just like to tell you how much I admire the way you've been handling the situation. And a lot of other people feel the same way."

It wasn't the promise of a job, nor was it even a hint of what management had in mind, but it was the nicest thing Luis had heard in ages.

"John made me feel so much better," Tiant recalls. "When he got up to leave, my spirit felt like flying again."

Contrary to the perennial expectations of their adoring public, the Red Sox failed to set the world on fire in the Grapefruit League season once again; indeed, their exhibition record was a disappointing 12–15.

That was one important factor in Tiant's shaky situation. The failure of the much-celebrated youth movement to pick up the club by its bootstraps had given Luis some breathing room.

But an even more significant development came on March 22 when the Sox traded relief pitcher Sparky Lyle to the Yankees for first baseman Danny Cater. Sparky had appeared in 50 games in 1971, posting a 6–4 record wih 16 saves and a respectable 2.77 ERA.

Though Tiant's overall 1971 record had been grim, there was a story within that story. In 11 relief appearances he had been 1–1 with a 1.80 ERA. And a partial rationalization of his total record might have been the fact that the Red Sox lineup produced fewer runs (2.45) for him than it did for any other Boston pitcher.

In any event, by the time spring training ended, Luis was a fixture in Kasko's bullpen plans.

"My idea was to keep him out there permanently," Eddie says. "If we ran into a problem with an unusually crowded schedule, or if someone became ill and unable to start at the last minute, then maybe Luis would be given a spot assignment. But his principal role was as a second-line pitcher, someone who could provide us with consistency in the middle innings."

It was in that capacity that Luis struck up a friendship with his southpaw counterpart, Bill Lee, a free spirit from USC who made no secret of his disdain for bullpen duty.

"There's status in baseball," Lee maintained, "and the relief pitcher ranks down at the bottom. Did you ever hear of anybody being sent out here as a reward?"

Lee was a constant source of exasperation for the staid old Boston front office. Like Longfellow's little girl who had a little curl right in the middle of her forehead, when Lee was good he was very, very good, but when he was bad he was horrid!

He was, for instance, one of the first Boston players who let their hair grow unconventionally long—at least by baseball's standards. A Red Sox coach suggested that some tonsorial repairs were in order. "I've got a lot of theories," Bill responded in a newspaper interview, "and one of them is that my hair does not affect my pitching. If people are looking for nice trim All-American boys, why don't they go to Quantico? Because hair has nothing to do with baseball. Suppose we all took our clothes off and ran onto the field. It would still be guys like Pete Rose who stood out. Do you know what I mean?"

Red Sox officials turned the other way and pretended not to listen, or to read, for Bill also happened to be a very valuable package of baseball talent. The Lord giveth and the Lord taketh away, they reminded themselves, and what He had given to Lee's left arm He apparently had deducted in the area of common sense. Lee, of course, thought it was the other way around. Pointing out that he possessed a degree from USC, he'd often ask, "What's an intelligent guy like me doing here?"

But no one competed harder than he did; no one was more intense about winning, or more upset with himself in defeat. In that respect Lee was thoroughly professional in management's eyes.

Small wonder, then, that he liked Luis right away.

"One thing I noticed about Luis," he says, "was that when things weren't going well he'd start working very, very hard. Once they got better, you could see he relaxed a bit. During that period when his future with the Red Sox seemed to be in jeopardy, he worked harder than anybody I'd ever seen before. And I'm talking about working on his own, doing it individually, like jogging 10 or 12 times around the ball park. Anybody who watched Luis that spring couldn't help rooting for him to come back all the way."

By the end of May Luis had appeared in nine games, including two spot starts, and his record was 0–1.

But in June he began to make a little bit of noise. It wasn't the type of thing you could pick out from the stands, nor did it inspire any enthusiasm in the media, but O'Connell, Sullivan and Kasko could sense something was happening, something good, something they had been crossing their fingers for all along. Luis made 10 appearances that month, nine in relief, and picked up his first two wins of the year. More important, however, was the fact that his ERA in that span was 1.80 and he was averaging a strikeout per inning. It was too soon to be patting themselves on the back, and yet they couldn't help smiling like the cat who ate the canary. If what they were beginning to suspect was indeed true, they'd soon be looking like sages to the rest of the baseball world.

On June 28 Luis pitched the final five innings of a 5–3 win over Detroit, allowing just one hit while striking out five.

On July 1 he picked up a save against Milwaukee.

Two days later, in a surprise starting role against the Twins (only his fourth start of the season), he went the entire nine innings and won, 8–2.

Four days after that, as the Sox opened a West Coast swing, he got credit for defeating the Angels, fanning three, walking none and yielding one hit after taking over with one out in the seventh.

Three days later the Sox were in Oakland, and young Lynn McGlothen tired in the ninth. With Boston holding a precarious 4–2 lead, he gave up a one-out double to Mike Epstein and then a line drive single to Bill Voss. Only Rick Miller's excellent defense kept Epstein from continuing on home. Kasko called time and then signaled for Luis, who'd be making his fifth appearance in 13 days. Oakland's top two RBI men were due up: Sal Bando and Dave Duncan.

"Kasko made a good move," Lee smiled later. "McGlothen was taking the ball from the catcher and then just firing it right back in there. They were getting used to him. But Luis would take the ball, hold it in his glove awhile, and then just stare at them. He was driving them nuts."

Bando popped up. Duncan, who had homered in each of his previous three games, then lined harmlessly to Miller in center.

Boston won, and Luis got the save.

In those five quick appearances Tiant had three wins and two saves.

"I can't recall another pitcher who had the mental approach to do all of the things Luis has done for us," Kasko told the Oakland press. "He's really been amazing in these last few games."

But the best was yet to come, and it was just around the corner.

CHAPTER 18

The Old Tiant Returns

As August got under way there was a feeling of excitement in Boston, not quite what you'd call pennant fever—although that was beginning to spread as well—but rather a much keener interest in the scores and standings of the American League East derby.

Since their "Impossible Dream" pennant of 1967, the Red Sox had dropped out of serious title contention. They continued to play winning baseball, but the closest they would come to a repeat performance in the next four seasons was their 86–76 record in 1968, which left them 17 games out of first place.

There was no reason to believe 1972 would be any different, especially after the Sox ended June eight games off the pace at 27–34.

But as July rolled along, they began to stir.

Sonny Siebert was scheduled to start against the Orioles on August 5, but a spell of dizziness made that impossible. So Kasko penciled in Tiant's name at the last minute, and Luis proceeded to go the distance, striking out six, walking none and beating Baltimore by a 6–3 score, thanks in large measure to Rico Petrocelli, who drove in all six runs.

One week later the two teams met again, this time in Baltimore, and Kasko decided to play a hunch.

"Luis," he asked, "can you beat these guys again?"

Tiant nodded. "Don't worry."

For six innings he kept the Orioles tied up in knots. Then Merv Rettemund opened the home half of the seventh with a triple, ending the bid for a no-hitter. Luis finally settled for a three-hit victory which boosted the Red Sox into third place, just 4½ games out of first.

He followed that effort with another relief job, then got his ninth starting assignment of the year when the traveling Red Sox pulled into Chicago. He had a no-hitter for five innings. Then six. Seven. The first two batters in the eighth went down, and now he was only four outs away from a piece of immortality. Carlos May took two fastballs for strikes, two knucklers for balls, then reached out and hit the 2–2 pitch down the left-field line for a double. The final score was Boston 3, Chicago 0. Luis ended up with nine strikeouts and a two-hitter.

Not only was it Tiant's second serious flirtation with a no-hitter, but also his third complete game in his last three starts.

"Ah, yes," Peter Gammons rhapsodized in his Boston *Globe* account of the game, "Luis Tiant, the reincarnation of a former pitcher named Luis Tiant, with his head bobbing, leg spastically kicking, and arms flailing, did it again yesterday. . . ."

Going into their meeting with Luis, the White Sox had won 20 out of 25 games, and their record at home had been an imposing 46–14. They would end the season with the second-best record in the entire American League. But on this particular day, against this particular man, they wouldn't even get a ball out of the infield until the sixth inning was almost over.

"This was a House of David game," Boston coach Eddie Popowski chirped. "You just give Luis the ball and then everybody has a good time while he wins again. He made it look that simple."

It came as no surprise, therefore, when Kasko completed his postgame analysis with a simple announcement to the assembled writers.

"Beginning right now," he smiled, "Luis Tiant is a starter."

On Friday night, August 25, the Sox returned to Fenway Park to open a nine-game home stand, and a wildly cheering crowd of 33,551—second-largest of the season—packed the house to welcome them back, and, more important, to lend support in what had rapidly become a very serious run at the pennant.

The starting nod went to Tiant, and Luis didn't disappoint the multitudes. With all of his spectacular repertoire in good working order—the spins, the stares, the tantalizing changeups, and the burning heat—he stopped the Texas Rangers cold, scattering four harmless hits and striking out nine. The final score was 4–0, his second shutout in a row.

Four days later the White Sox arrived in Boston, still a bit miffed over the way Tiant embarrassed them at home the previous week. But they soon discovered it hadn't been a fluke, for Luis shut them out again, 5–0, with a three-hitter that hoisted Boston up into third place, just three games away from the top.

Luis had now thrown three shutouts in a row. In those 27 innings he struck out 23, walked only three and gave up a total of 11 hits.

"He's as good as any pitcher in the league right now," White Sox manager Chuck Tanner marveled. "He was like a surgeon out there tonight. It was really something to see."

But Tanner couldn't possibly have enjoyed the show as much as Kasko, the man who believed in Tiant before it became a popular thing to do.

"You just sit back and watch him go," Eddie grinned when writers sought out scraps of strategy to include in their stories. "He's positively amazing. A truly great pitcher."

Tiant's record for the month of August had been 5–0, with an almost unbelievable ERA of 0.94!

The Red Sox, meanwhile, were in the thick of the race, only two games out of first place as the month of September began.

That margin had shrunk to one game when Luis made his next appearance, against the Brewers in Milwaukee's County Stadium. And he maintained it with still another superlative effort, holding the Brewers to five meaningless hits as Boston coasted to its eighth win in nine tries, 2–0.

Luis now had four consecutive shutouts, spanning a string of 36 consecutive scoreless innings in which he had struck out 31, walked seven, and allowed 16 hits.

"He's exactly the same pitcher he was in 1968," Sonny Siebert told the writers. "The only difference is that if he had thrown four shutouts for the Indians he would have ended up 2–2 instead of 4–0!"

The fact was, however, that he did throw four consecutive shutouts for Cleveland in 1968, and was well on his way to a fifth against the Orioles when Boog Powell, jammed by a fastball, hit a broken-bat homer down the right-field line in the seventh inning with Luis leading, 2–0.

"If we make it into the World Series this year," reliever Ken Tatum suggested, "Luis ought to get two shares."

There were no more disbelievers left, no more doubters to be found.

But there were plenty of observers still scratching their heads over the resurrection that had taken place before their eyes.

Ray Fitzgerald went so far as to write a tongue-in-cheek *mea culpa* in his next Boston *Globe* column: "I can remember writing in May, 'Goodbye, Luis Tiant, and Bob Bolin makes two.' Now Tiant is a sensation, and Bolin is the number one reliever, and nobody is after me to manage in the major leagues. . . ."

On September 7 the Red Sox moved into first place by hauling the Yankees over the coals at Fenway Park, 10–4. It was the first time they had been in that position in more than a year, dating back to June 1971.

On September 8 Luis—trying for his fifth shutout in a row— kept the Yanks at bay for four innings, then allowed a double to Felipe Alou and a run-producing single up the middle to Celerino Sanchez (at whose 1971 wedding, ironically, Luis served as best man). That ended Tiant's string of consecutive scoreless innings at 40⅓. As Luis began warming up prior to the start of the sixth inning, the crowd of 28,462 stood and gave him a rousing ovation. He finished with a four-hit, 4–2 victory, his seventh win in a row.

"I don't care about the shutout," he insisted. "All I care about is winning."

And he was doing plenty of that with an 11–4 record and a 2.07 ERA.

The Yankees finally derailed him down in New York the following week by a 3–2 margin; then Luis went out and hurled *two more shutouts*. The first was a 10–0 rout of the Indians, who could muster only three hits off of their onetime ace. Home runs by Tommy Harper, Carl Yastrzemski, Doug Griffin and Carlton Fisk made the contest a lark.

But everyone knew his next appearance was going to be an entirely different proposition.

When the New York Yankees won the 1964 American League pennant race, it was symbolic that their final margin was just one game over Chicago and two games over Baltimore. It was their fifth league championship in a row, their ninth in 10 years, their fourteenth in 16 years, their twenty-ninth in 44 years! And it was also their last gasp, signaling the end of an historic dynasty that had inspired both awe and abhorrence from three generations of American audiences.

The league—indeed, the game—breathed easier following the Yanks' demise, as if an interminable cloud had finally passed overhead.

Minnesota won the American League title in 1965. Baltimore copped it in 1966. Four teams went into the last week of 1967's race with a good shot at the title before Boston finally prevailed on the final day of the schedule. Detroit surfaced to claim the 1968 championship. It was never like this in the days of Ruth and Gehrig, of DiMaggio and Henrich, of Mantle and Berra.

Then a new menace arrived in 1969. The Baltimore Orioles won 109 games that season, finishing 15 games ahead of Detroit. They won 108 in 1970, finishing 15 games ahead of New York. And they won 101 in 1971, a solid 12 games ahead of Detroit. Clearly, they were the finest team in all of baseball, even though they lost two of their three World Series.

But now, as the 1972 race headed into a spectacular home-stretch, the Orioles found themselves chasing not one, but two divisional rivals. The Tigers and the Red Sox were neck-and-neck for first place, with the O's nipping at their heels. Time was rapidly running out for Baltimore, however, making its three-game visit to Fenway Park of paramount importance.

The Orioles jumped all over young Lynn McGlothen in Game 1, 5–2. Then rain forced postponement of Game 2 in the series, so a doubleheader was set for Wednesday, September 20. When Marty Pattin, in perhaps his finest hour with the Bosox, beat Jim Palmer, 9–1, in the opener, the O's realized they were in serious trouble. They *had* to win the nightcap if they were to salvage the series. In Mike Cuellar (17–10) they were confident they had the right man to stop the Red Sox juggernaut.

The fans were just beginning to file back to their seats for the rematch, all refreshed and relieved, and the swarm of writers up in the press box were jotting down starting lineups when Luis Tiant completed his warmups, slung a jacket over his shoulder, closed the bullpen gate behind him, and began the long trek across the outfield on his way to the Boston dugout.

It was 8:10 P.M.

"The noise started in center field," Larry Claflin recalled in his Boston *Herald American* column the next day. "Then it quickly spread along the right-field line. At first, we in the press box didn't realize what it was all about. Then we understood. They were cheering Tiant. . . . As Tiant strode across the field, the noise grew and grew. The 28,777 fans stood and cheered his every step. . . ."

By the time Luis arrived at the dugout his teammates were waiting to greet him, caught up in the spontaneous outpouring of respect and admiration that now rolled across the ball park in waves and waves of thunderous applause.

"That's the kind of thing you just love to see in sports," said John Kennedy, the popular utility infielder who became known as "Super Sub" that season. "It had nothing whatsoever to do with me personally, yet I was thrilled to death watching Luis walk across the field in the middle of that tribute. My heart was pounding and I could actually feel tears in my eyes. And I know that every guy in that dugout felt the same way I did. It was one of the most thrilling scenes I've ever witnessed."

But it was only a prelude. As the game progressed and Luis continued to baffle the Orioles with his very best assortment of skill and skulduggery, the crowd began responding to his every move. "They even roared with approval one time when he reached down to pick up the resin," Boston *Globe* writer Neil Singelais reported. It was more than just exuberance over winning a key game; it was a declaration of gratitude, from a town so often disappointed to a man so often counted out. Now both were going to get their just rewards.

By the bottom of the eighth inning everyone knew the game was over. The Orioles had been held to four harmless hits while the Sox had pushed four runs across the plate. Now Tiant got up from the on-deck circle and made his way to the batter's box, but Sherm Feller's introduction over the public-address system was drowned out by the tumultuous standing ovation that followed Luis step by step and pitch by pitch, for the crowd continued to roar all the while he stood at the plate; and then it returned to its feet to noisily salute his every delivery in the ninth until the Orioles had finally been laid to rest, 4–0.

"It made me feel funny inside," Luis remembers. "I kept thinking it was the biggest night of my life. It made me want to cry out there."

"I have never heard an ovation like that," Larry Claflin continued in his column, "except perhaps for the last time Joe DiMaggio went to bat in Boston, or Bob Cousy's final game."

Indeed, any accurate description of what took place that night at Fenway Park only invites charges of overstatement and gross sentimentality. You simply had to be there to understand.

"I've never heard anything like that in my life," Carl Yastrzemski said. "But I'll tell you one thing: Tiant deserved every bit of it."

It was Commander Oliver Hazard Perry, standing on the deck of the *Niagara,* dispatching the terse report to General William Henry Harrison: *"We have met the enemy, and they are ours."* Standing on the mound at Fenway that night, Luis could have made the same claim. He had met the three-time league champions, and they were his.

"He really showed me something tonight," Baltimore outfielder Terry Crowley marveled. "I don't think I ever saw a pitcher who could work from behind any better than Luis did out there just now. That's when he's at his best, throwing you a 2–0 pitch that's almost impossible to hit. Before you know it, he's ahead of you again."

Boog Powell had the proper word for it. "Gutsy," the big man said. "That guy's as gutsy as they come. That was the *old Tiant* we were watching. He's as good as he ever was."

The next day Billy Martin arrived in Boston with his Detroit Tigers and writers advised him of what had just transpired. "I'm not surprised," Billy shrugged. "I still remember Ron Perranoski calling me last year and telling me to take this guy. If things had been different, maybe I would have. But I already had two questionable arms on my staff. There was no room for a third."

Detroit drew first blood in the four-game showdown, 10–3. Boston won the second, 3–2. Then the Tigers romped again as Mickey Lolich won his twenty-first, 7–1.

Now it was Tiant's turn again.

And he made Perranoski look like a prophet in Martin's eyes, turning back the Tigers, 7–2, for his third complete game win in nine days.

That kept the Red Sox in first place, one game ahead of Detroit.

Five days later the team pulled into Baltimore, and Luis was sent out in Game 1. He was the last guy the Orioles wanted to see, for now their backs were flat against the wall. One more loss would mathematically eliminate them from the race. It was no surprise, therefore, that manager Earl Weaver called upon his ace, Jim Palmer (21–9), to solve the Tiant mystery. Luis had beaten them three times in three tries so far.

For nine innings they battled on even terms, and at the end of the regulation contest they were deadlocked, 2–2. Then in the top of the tenth, Yastrzemski (who had hit five home runs in earlier Tiant games) drove a two-run shot into the stands, guaranteeing that a new American League representative would be going to the World Series this time.

The win gave Luis a 15–5 record, a phenomenal total for a man who didn't get his first start until June 21 and had only three starts altogether as of July 3. From August 19 through that elimination of the Orioles on September 29, Luis was 9–1, with six shutouts and an ERA of 0.96. And all of the wins were complete games.

"What this man has accomplished is the most remarkable thing I've ever been associated with," Kasko said. "And boy, does he deserve it. He never lost faith in himself, not even when he was 1–7 last year."

But there was still the matter of a pennant race to be resolved.

That players strike in springtime had come back to haunt the American League East in autumn. As the Red Sox flew into Detroit for a face-to-face showdown with the Tigers, they had a half-game lead in the standings, but that was a negligible advantage. For practical purposes, Boston (84–68) and Detroit (84–69) were dead even, both needing two wins to nail down the divisional championship. There was no way the Tigers, who had a 156-game schedule, and the Sox, whose schedule contained 155, could end up tied. Of course, anyone suggesting such an unlikely photo finish back in April would have been summarily dismissed as an alarmist, for, after all, who the hell was going to be able to stop Baltimore?

But, alas, it all came down to three games in the Motor City.

The Tigers moved to a quick 1–0 lead in the first game, but the Sox rallied in the third. With Harper and Luis Aparicio on base, Yastrzemski lined a single up the middle. Tommy scored easily, knotting the score at 1–1, and Aparicio was waved in behind him with what should have been the go-ahead run. But as he sped past third, his right foot caught the top of the bag, jarring him off balance. As he stumbled forward he slipped on wet grass, thus becoming an easy target for the pickoff throw which killed the rally. It was the last chance the Sox would get from Mickey Lolich. He ended up with 15 strikeouts and his twenty-second victory, and the Tigers ended up with a half-game lead.

That left it squarely up to Tiant in Game 2.

Following a late-afternoon steak with his roommate, Harper, Luis arrived at the ball park and took an eight-minute rubdown from trainer Buddy LeRoux. Harold Kaese, the late Boston *Globe* columnist, shared Bill Lee's previously mentioned observation. "He looked little like baseball royalty," Kaese wrote. "Stocky, thick-chested, short-armed: this was one of the princes of pitching?" Returning to the locker room, Luis spotted a mechanical monkey sitting by John Kennedy's locker. The monkey banged cymbals until its head was tapped; then it stopped and began to squeal. Luis smiled and walked over.

"He got it going," Kaese wrote, "then laughed. He slapped it on the head and laughed again. All the players in the room stopped dressing, talking, pounding their gloves, trimming their pant legs, stretching their caps; they looked at Tiant and the monkey and they began to laugh with him."

Kaese was fascinated by the seeming lack of concern on Tiant's part. The whole nation was tuned in for what promised to be the most critical game of the year, and here was Luis going into hysterics as he slapped a mechanical monkey around to the delight of his equally jovial mates.

"Aren't you nervous?" Harold finally asked.

"Me?" Luis smiled. "No. It's another game, that's all. I might win or I might lose, but it's not going to help to get nervous."

For five innings he held the Tigers at bay. In the fifth they managed to get two men on with one out, but Luis hummed three quick fastballs past Al Kaline and then got a big assist from rookie outfielder Dwight Evans, who caught the third out from a prone position after a great run.

Two walks, a sacrifice, and Jim Northrup's single allowed Detroit to tie the game, 1–1, in the sixth. A Dick McAuliffe double and a Kaline single put the Tigers ahead, 2–1, an inning later.

The final score was 3–1. Two of the runs were unearned. Boston had just four hits, one of them by Tiant.

Reporters entering the Red Sox locker room were struck by the unabashed emotions they encountered. Many of the Boston players, long accused of being overpaid and lackadaisical, were sobbing quietly. Carlton Fisk, the outstanding young catcher who would soon become the league's first unanimous Rookie of the Year, sat hunched in front of his locker, crying and clenching his fists, as Tom Yawkey—the beloved owner of the team—gently patted his shoulder. Yastrzemski, brushing away tears, called it "the biggest disappointment of my life."

Later that night, after the reporters and cameramen had departed and some of the players had begun heading back to their hotel, two men talked alone in the trainer's room.

"Goddamn it," Eddie Kasko said, extending his hand, "you had one hell of a year."

Tiant shook the hand warmly and nodded. It had been on his mind to say something to this man when the season ended, but tonight he wasn't quite prepared. He hadn't expected it would end this way. Earlier in the season an illness struck the family down in Mexico City. Few people in Boston knew about it, but Kasko heard the story and beckoned Luis into his office. "If I can loan you some money or anything like that to help," he said, "just let me know. It'll be between you and me." Luis never forgets things like that. Nor did he ever forget the many times Kasko went out of his way to defend him against critics in the media, especially during those trying days in 1971 when his career seemed to hang in the balance.

He looked at Kasko and smiled.

"Thanks, Skip. You're my man."

Luis was the American League's ERA champ with his 1.91 mark, becoming the first Boston pitcher to claim that honor since Mel Parnell in 1949, and the first Red Sox pitcher with an ERA under 2.00 since Carl Mays in 1917. It was, of course, his second time leading the league. The first was in 1968 at Cleveland, when his figure was 1.60.

To no one's surprise, he was a shoo-in as the league's Comeback Player of the Year.

In his 21 winning appearances (both starting and relieving), he had an ERA of 0.95.

And in Fenway Park, long considered a hitter's paradise, he won his last 10 games in a row.

"In this business you take your chances," Dick O'Connell says. "You have to take chances on guys who have the potential to do well, and then hope they do it. If they don't, you're stupid. If they do, you're a genius."

And what about getting Luis Tiant?

O'Connell smiled. "A stroke of genius."

PART V
The Superstar

PART two

The Superior

CHAPTER 19

Tommy's Tutors

Tommy Harper never missed the limelight in his previous 10 seasons as a major leaguer, perhaps because he never sought it. Anonymity had been easy to come by during his five summers in Cincinnati, thanks to his more illustrious teammates, and all of the attention in Cleveland during his one year there (1968) had been focused on Tiant's great 21–9 performance.

Then in 1969 he became the only star of the expansion Seattle team as he led the major leagues in stolen bases with 73. The following season he became one of only five players in American League history to hit at least 30 home runs (31) and steal at least 30 bases (38) in the same year.

"But I always felt I'd rather be part of a championship team somewhere else than be a star on a losing ball club," he says. "I just couldn't accept the idea of doing interviews every day, saying the same things over and over, answering the same old obvious questions each time a writer came over to see me. Really, the idea of being a star never turned me on."

He was delighted when Milwaukee (nee Seattle) traded him to Boston in 1972, and now as the 1973 season got under way he was confident—along with millions of New Englanders—that those championship aspirations were at last within reach. But first he had to make some adjustments. Toward the end of the 1972 race with Detroit, the Sox moved Golden Glove left fielder Yastrzemski in to cover first base, mainly because of a gimpy knee, and he remained there through the dramatic conclusion of the schedule. Now there was talk of making the switch a permanent one, especially with so many strong young arms (Dwight Evans, Cecil Cooper, Rick Miller, et al.) abounding on the roster.

Harper would get first crack at the job, even though the word around Boston was that his defense was a liability. His principal role had been leadoff batter, and he was excellent in that capacity throughout 1972, reaching base in 126 of his 144 games and leading the team in scoring with 92 runs. He also stole 25 bases, reviving what had become a lost art at Fenway Park. Kasko had to keep him in the 1973 lineup, and so Tommy found himself shifted from center to left as the campaign began.

Tiant was bothered by the flak his friend received in the field, not just because he liked Tommy, but also because he felt that the criticism was unfair. He knew from their days together in Cleveland that Harper could track down fly balls with most of his major league peers. Indeed, one night in Chicago Luis got into early trouble when two White Sox batters reached base in the first inning. Tom McCraw followed with a booming shot down the right-field line, headed for the bleachers. But Tommy dove into the stands and caught it, costing McCraw a three-run homer. Luis went on to pitch a shutout, for which he was given a certificate good for a new suit. He gave the certificate to Tommy. "That's the kind of guy he is," Harper says.

But now Tommy was catching hell from the media.

"I don't understand this," Luis told him one day after reading a Boston column chastising Tommy's defensive work in left. "You're a good fielder."

"Hey," Harper explained, "you can't stop them from writing. Who knows how these things get started? Someone says something about you, and the next thing you know you're trying to live it down."

Still, it rankled Luis, enough so that he pulled Yastrzemski aside one day.

"Tommy's catching hell," he said. "Why don't you see if you can help him; maybe tell him some things about the wall."

The Wall! Affectionately known as the Green Monster! Lurking an inviting 315 feet away from home plate at Fenway Park, the famed left-field barrier stands 37 feet high, topped by a 23-foot screen. It's always mentioned as a factor when hitter goes against pitcher, but no one is more aware of its presence (and potential horrors) than the fielder stationed in its shadows. If he plays with his back against it, there's an excellent chance a fly ball will strike the surface just above his head and then carom wildly out of his reach. But if he plays shallow, guarding against the carom, there's an equally good chance the ball will end up hitting three feet off the ground, making him look like a perfect fool in front of 30,000 unsympathetic judges. Throw in the wind and the sun and a handful of other variables, and you understand why left field in Boston is sometimes seen as baseball's version of Valhalla, the hall of the slain.

But Yastrzemski was the exception. With his gifts of perception, speed and agility, he played the Wall like Chopin played a polonaise. He was the master, and now Luis asked him to be the teacher, too.

"You don't have to have the strongest arm in the world to be a good outfielder," Yaz explained to Tommy one day as the two of them, accompanied by Tiant, walked out to left field for a conference. "The important thing is to be accurate. And you've got to be aggressive, not defensive. That's the biggest thing of all. Forget about making errors. Don't even think about that. And don't listen to the people in the stands. You can't play safety first out here. You've got to come in on the ball. With your speed you should be charging every one of them. If you catch it, you catch it. And if you miss it, so what? If the ball's hit hard enough to get past you, the man on third would have scored anyway. But the guy on first still has to hold up until he sees how far away from you it lands. Just learn to relax and do your thing, and you'll have no problems."

Harper was never mentioned for a Golden Glove that season, but he did begin playing well enough to silence his critics. Near the end of September, in fact, the statistics told the story of his improvement.

"Look," he said, poking Tiant's shoulder as he flashed the latest stat sheet. "See that? Eleven men thrown out. I'm leading the club!"

"You should be leading," Luis replied, blowing a puff of cigar smoke at the paper in Tommy's hands. "The way everybody kept running on you, you must have had 100 chances!"

With newly acquired Orlando Cepeda starring in the designated hitter role (20 homers, 86 RBI), it was imperative that Harper make the grade as a fielder, for his base running was soon to become an integral part of the Boston attack. He didn't need any special coaching in this department, as his 73 steals of 1969 amply demonstrated, but that didn't stop him from going to Luis one day for a private tutoring session on the mound.

"When you're in your stretch, can you really see the runner on first?" he asked. "If I stand here and try to throw, I can't see what's happening over there unless I turn my head and look."

"That's right," Luis nodded. "You can't really see the man's lead."

"Then how do you know when to throw over there?"

"I don't. At least not all the time. Look. Here's my stretch. I'm just trying to peer over there, see? But I can't really tell how far off the bag he is. Sometimes I throw just because I know the man is fast. But if I don't look first, I can't really be sure where he is."

Harper had suspected as much, but this confirmation was reassuring. In the never-ending battle of nerves between base runner and pitcher, it helped to have an edge, to accurately surmise what was going through the other fellow's mind.

"Luis helped me a lot," Tommy remembers. "He showed me little things to look for, things a runner might not be aware of. I got to the point where I could really analyze a pitcher. If he didn't turn his head in my direction, then I knew he could be caught off guard. Plus we discussed balance. The thing that makes Luis so good on pickoffs is the way he picks just the right second to fire the ball at you. You can be just one foot off the bag, but if your feet are in the wrong position when he throws, it's almost like being paralyzed. You simply can't react fast enough. Luis catches a lot of runners that way. That's why you won't see too many players taking chances against him."

By season's end, Harper would become the greatest base runner in Red Sox history.

CHAPTER 20

A 20-Game Winner

Luis wasn't sharp in his 1973 debut, but he didn't have to be, thanks to a devastating Boston assault on New York pitching, 15–5.

A week later, in his second outing, he faced the Yanks again, and this time he looked like the Tiant of ERA fame as he held them to three hits and a run before he tired in the ninth and had to be relieved. Harper almost saved that run by diving into the Yankee Stadium seats in fruitless pursuit of Felipe Alou's solo homer in the second. So Luis had a 3–1 victory, his one hundredth major league triumph, ironically occurring in the same park where he made his big league debut by shutting out Mantle, Maris and company nine years earlier.

But, true to his well-established pattern of starting slowly in the coolness of the springtime, he proceeded to get bounced around in his next two appearances.

Then came one of those epic Tiant performances, on Saturday, April 28, in Fenway Park against the White Sox. He rang up 11 strikeouts, including three against a totally frustrated Dick Allen. "He just slices batters apart," catcher Fisk raved to reporters. "The whole idea of good hitting is timing, rhythm and concentration. A guy like Allen wants to get up there and go to work right away, so Luis will stand out there and stare at him for what seems like an hour. You can hear Allen cursing. One time he looked at me and said, 'This guy's putting me to sleep!' Luis knows the hitters better than anyone else in the business, and when he goes to work on them he's like a surgeon."

But the rest of his operating team wasn't as precise. Indeed, the Bosox played erratically in the field and stranded 16 runners on the bases, practically gift wrapping a 2–1 Chicago victory.

"It's a good thing Luis Tiant's language isn't decipherable sometimes," Clif Keane observed in the next day's Boston *Globe*. He had been one of several writers who tried unsuccessfully to ferret Tiant's postgame feelings.

"I don't want to talk to anybody!" Luis fumed, kicking a chair on his way to the whirlpool.

Four days later the Texas Rangers arrived in Boston and were greeted by more of Tiant's mastery as he fanned eight, walked none and breezed to a 6–2 decision, after which he willingly reviewed each highlight for a crowd of writers. The lively conference prevented Harper from getting to his locker, which was adjacent to Tiant's.

"Hey, Yaz," Tommy asked loudly, "isn't that the same guy who wasn't going to talk to reporters anymore?" Carl laughed, and so did everyone else, except for Luis, who was too preoccupied explaining every detail of this latest conquest.

Luis was still blowing hot and cold, however, much like the weather which seemed to bother him so much each year as he made the transition from the sunny atmosphere of the South to the windswept cities of the North. Most ballplayers view July and August as the dog days, those steamy afternoons when each drop of perspiration appears to carry off another ounce of strength. But Tiant's system thrives on heat, making it as different from the norm as his style is.

On May 11 he beat the Indians handily; on the sixteenth he lost to the Tigers, allowing nine hits; on the twenty-first he toyed with the Orioles, winning an easy four-hitter; six days later Kansas City climbed all over him, 13–3; then he concluded the month in grand style with a 2–1 win over the Angels in which he struck out nine.

He was as consistent as Jell-O.

The win over the Angels was marred by two bench-clearing incidents. The trouble began when Rudy Meoli tapped a grounder back to the mound. Luis scooped up the ball and faked a throw home, then whirled and fired a strike toward third. Alan Gallagher, the runner on third, had been clearly caught off guard and now was in the midst of a rundown. He was flustered, and he proceeded to take it out on Fisk, whom he knocked head over heels with unnecessary gusto. When Gallagher reappeared at the plate in the seventh, Tiant sent him a message in the form of a fastball that whistled past him, high and inside. Moments later Gallagher and Fisk were swapping angry words, bringing both squads out on the double. The scene was repeated in the bottom of the inning when pitcher Clyde Wright's first offering sailed over Danny Cater's head.

"I wasn't throwing at him," Luis explained later. "I just wanted to let him know that Fisk is on my side. When he fights with Fisk, he fights with me, too."

That homely bit of philosophy would have horrified the Marquis of Queensberry, but in baseball it's generally accepted as an article of faith, and no doubt even Gallagher went along with Luis' reasoning—once he realized his right ear was still where it belonged.

By the end of May, Tiant's record was 6–5.

In June he continued the same uneven pace, winning two and losing three. One of the losses was a 12–1 embarrassment at the hands of the Athletics. One of the wins was a splendid four-hitter against those same Athletics.

By the end of June he was 8–8.

And then he began to roll, winning his first four starts in July, highlighted by a two-hitter against the Twins.

"The weather," he said, "does mean a lot to me."

By the end of July he was 13–9, and suddenly a 20-victory season seemed within reach.

He threw 10 strikeouts to beat Baltimore for his fourteenth win, then later that week beat Kansas City for No. 15.

Eddie Kasko will never forget that particular win in Baltimore.

"I think most managers are prone to worry during every game," Eddie says. "From inning to inning, from hitter to hitter, from pitch to pitch, there's always something to be concerned about.

But Luis could relieve you of much of that concern when he was going right—like in that '72 homestretch, for example. Every time I sat down with my coaches to figure out the pitching rotation for a particular series, we'd come to Tiant's name and relax. You just knew when it was his turn to go, he'd give you nine good innings. You could count on a good job every time.

"Anyway, this night we were getting ready to play the Orioles down in Baltimore, and for some reason I had Earl Williams on my mind. Earl is always a fear for opposing managers because he can bust a game wide open any time. So I'm sitting on the bench with Luis and I happen to mention Earl's name. 'Don't let him beat you on a fastball,' I told him. Luis just looked at me with a smile and said, 'Williams? That big donkey? Maybe I'll strike him out three times!'

"Well, he struck him out the first time. And struck him out again in the fifth. Then he got him on a little grounder in the seventh.

"So as he started to go out in the ninth inning I said, 'Luis, you've used up every move in the book. What in hell are you going to throw him this time?' He laughed and said, 'Don't worry, I'll think of something.'

"So he gets two strikes on Earl. Then just before delivering his next pitch, he gave it one of those crazy Tiant moves—you know, wiggling the glove, nodding his head, and finally releasing a breaking ball from way down sidearm somewhere! Poor Williams. His butt flew out and he swung with all his might, but Luis had him again."

Kasko joined the rest of the Sox in the traditional reception committee atop the dugout steps, and as soon as Luis arrived, Eddie extended his hand.

"Goddamn it," he said, "you did think of something, didn't you?"

Although Baltimore was back in its customary driver's seat following its 1972 hiatus, the Red Sox were still in contention when they opened a mid-August series against Oakland at Fenway Park.

Luis was Kasko's choice to work the opener. Boston was just 2½ games out of first. This was Tiant's favorite stage, a tough opponent in a key game on a hot night in Boston. And he was equal to the task once again, fanning nine A's, but the Red Sox failed to give him any support, resulting in a 3–1 defeat.

Muscle spasms in his lower back caused him to miss his next two starts. When he returned to duty on August 26 in Anaheim against the California Angels, the Sox were still in the race, although they had slipped to four games behind the front-running Orioles. Luis pitched magnificently, but once again the Boston bats were silent. He lost, 1–0, though allowing only three hits.

It was the sixth time that season he had been given one run—or no runs—to work with.

Five days later he faced the Brewers in Milwaukee and pitched a four-hitter, striking out nine. And again he lost, 3–2.

In addition to frittering away their pennant possibilities, the Sox were also jeopardizing Tiant's bid for a 20-victory season. He had just pitched three superb games and lost them all, leaving him with a 15–12 record as the schedule moved into September.

When all of his losses were analyzed at the end of the season, it would be revealed that his teammates had scored an average of 1.77 runs in those frustrating setbacks. It was almost like Cleveland revisited.

But another facet of this unique personality began to surface, one that teammates were quick to observe.

"Luis never bitches when the guys behind him make errors in the field or fail to get a hit," Stan Williams says. "He's got a remarkable attitude in those situations. He'll get mad at himself, but not at the other players. This is so important to a team. If a player thinks the pitcher is going to jump all over him for a mistake, he ends up playing scared. It makes him tense. And that's what causes errors a lot of times. Luis is a real professional, and they all appreciate it."

It was a trait Yastrzemski admired.

"All Luis cares about is winning," Carl explains. "He doesn't give a damn about statistics. I've watched him walk over to someone who's just made an error—even an error that cost him a shutout—and tell the guy not to worry about it. That's why everyone loves to play behind him. He's really a super guy, a class player all the way."

That's not to say Tiant is an entirely carefree performer, however.

Bill Lee, in his own inimitable fashion, attempted to explore the approach Luis brings to a game from an amateur psychologist's point of view.

"Here's where Luis and I are different," he suggests. "I get upset when I make a terrible pitch because I strive for perfection. But if I make a good pitch and the guy still gets a hit, it doesn't bother me. I figure there was nothing I could do about it. You see, I can attain perfection and still lose the ball game.

"But Luis—he's just win, win, win. It's his whole life. It's an inbred thing.

"I don't want to fail out there. I'm afraid of failing. I'm not afraid to lose; I'm afraid to fail. You see, losing and failing are not the same things to me.

"But Luis thinks he's failed if he loses.

"I've trained my mind to take the animal fears that he and I both feel and convert them to mental feelings.

"That's the only difference between Luis and me as far as our competitive natures are concerned."

That's also why young reporters in need of a quick, incisive postgame analysis are usually advised to avoid Lee's locker, lest they spend the next three hours trying to unravel their thoughts.

But Bill's observations notwithstanding, there's really nothing complicated about Luis' coolness under fire.

"You can't always go looking for people to blame," he shrugs. "That's something every ballplayer should learn when he's young. As long as I know the other guys are trying as hard as I am, how can I get mad at them for making a mistake or not getting a hit? When I give up a home run no one gives me hell, do they? It's no different. You've got to learn how to accept that. I've learned that much in my career. You can say I've learned a lot about life in my career, I guess."

It was obvious, even to the most diehard Red Sox rooters, that Boston wasn't going to win the divisional title after all. The cream had come to the top, as it always does, and once again the Orioles had proven they were the cream of the American League East.

But there was still plenty of excitement in Fenway Park as the month of September began, and most of it emanated from those two bosom buddies, Harper and Tiant.

After learning to deal with the intricacies of the Wall in April and May, Tommy found himself benched in June for lack of hitting. His average had dropped to .224, leaving Kasko no choice but to remove him from the lineup.

"No, I don't like the idea at all," Harper told a writer, "but how can I complain? Managers don't bench .300 hitters. If I had the hits, I'd be out there. It's my own fault I'm sitting here. I don't have to ask why I'm not playing. I know why. Sometimes there are exceptions, guys who do other things well enough to compensate for not hitting. But when you're the leadoff batter you're expected to get on base. If you don't, you're hurting the team. It's as simple as that. And I've been hurting this team."

In the second week of July, Kasko returned him to the leadoff spot, and Tommy proceeded to play the most exciting baseball of his life. In those remaining 10 weeks he batted .324, hitting 14 of his 17 homers and collecting 48 of his 71 RBI.

But it wasn't his bat—and surely not his glove—that had the fans on their feet at Fenway in the closing weeks of the season. Harper had them cheering for stolen bases, and that was surely a novelty for Boston patrons who had come to regard the stolen base much the same was as ornithologists view the bald eagle. Consider, for instance, that Gene Stephens and Pete Runnels led the Red Sox in that category with five steals apiece in 1960. Yastrzemski and Dalton Jones shared the lead in 1964 with six each. As late as 1971 the lead was held by Doug Griffin and Reggie Smith, both of whom stole 11. Faster than a speeding bullet? Hardly.

Then Tommy arrived in 1972 and stole 25. It was a paltry total by his high standards, but around Kenmore Square in modern times the only guys who ran that fast were being chased by cops.

And now, as 1973 wound down, he was actually battling Oakland's Bill North for the American League lead. The pace began unobtrusively. In a midseason game against Cleveland, for example, Tommy resisted an easy steal. "I was on second and there was nobody within 10 feet of me," he recalls. "I could have stolen third with no trouble. But we were leading 16–7. It wouldn't have made any sense. All I'd have been doing was rubbing it in, kind of like in basketball when guys come in at the end and score a lot of garbage points."

But once it became apparent that he was bearing down on the all-time Red Sox record of 52, set by the immortal Tris Speaker in 1912, Tommy began stealing in earnest. If and when he broke the record, club officials announced, the game would be halted and Harper would be presented with the base.

"In that case," he grinned, "I'm going to try stealing home. I want to stand there while they dig it up."

He ended up with second base on his trophy shelf at home. He also ended up with a total of 54, one better than Bill North.

"That," Bill Lee insisted, "is the way to play this game."

But one member of the team was clearly unimpressed, or so it seemed.

"If they ever trade you," Luis warned Tommy while the rest of the Sox broke into laughing, "don't you ever try to steal on me. First of all, you probably wouldn't even get a chance unless I walked you because you can't hit me. But don't ever try to. You know what I'll do?"

Tiant reached over and poked his forefinger into Harper's mouth.

"If I ever pick you off, I'm going to walk right over to first base and hook you by the mouth, just like this, and say: 'Get your ass out of here; you are *out!*' "

"You know something?" Tommy grins. "He would do it."

It appeared that Luis would be victimized by poor support for the fourth consecutive game as he dueled with Baltimore's Jim Palmer on September 4 at Fenway. Through nine innings the clubs had fought to a 1–1 stalemate, but now the Orioles had loaded the bases with no outs in the tenth. Then Luis got Rich Coggins to ground to first, where Cecil Cooper began a crisp 3–2–3 double play, and retired Paul Blair on a weak roller to third to escape unscathed. But Palmer was working with routine invincibility as the contest dragged on through the eleventh. Then, after retiring 16 batters in a row, he made a mistake as he led off the twelfth and young Ben Oglivie hoisted his first pitch into the left-field net, giving Luis a hard-earned 2–1 victory. It was his twentieth complete game, a new personal high, and it jumped his record to 16–12 with five starts remaining.

A week later he met the Orioles again and needed relief help to hold onto his seventeenth win, 4–3.

Then he beat Cleveland, 6–4, for No. 18.

The Yankees made him work, even though they got only four hits off of him, including Graig Nettles' homer, which deprived him of his first 1973 shutout. Roy White opened the ninth with a line drive into right field, but Luis recovered to strike out Thurmon Munson and Bobby Murcer after getting Mike Hegan on a pop-up. Now he was 19–12.

"I don't usually give a damn about records," he admitted to Boston writers, "but every pitcher would like to win 20. And now I've got a chance."

On most days the five-hitter he tossed at the Tigers would have been sufficient, but Joe Coleman threw a one-hitter at the Sox, handing Tiant his first loss in five games.

He had one last chance, September 28 against Milwaukee in Boston, and it turned out to be a laugher. He struck out nine, Yastrzemski contributed a grand slam, and Harper brought the proceedings to a halt when he stole his fifty-third base, breaking the Speaker record.

The final score was 11–2, and Luis had his twentieth win.

"I brought this thing to Detroit with me," he beamed, pointing to the foot-long stogie in his mouth, "and then I had to cart it all the way back here again. But it still tastes good. Now I'm tired. I'm going to take a long rest."

CHAPTER 21

Fish, Dogs and Toilets

Carl Yastrzemski couldn't have been any happier if he'd gone five-for-five. As the most avid fisherman on the ball club he took a lot of ribbing, but now he hoped to silence the disbelievers by showing them the prize catch he had just pulled out of the waters of Winter Haven.

"How do you like this beauty?" he asked, displaying it proudly to a gathering group of Boston players as he waited for their congratulations.

The first voice emanated from the rear of the crowd, a high-pitched squeal. "It's got teeth like Harper's!" Tiant shouted, and within an instant a plan was being formulated.

"When I came into the clubhouse," Tommy recalls, "I sort of sensed everyone was too quiet. Then I looked over toward my locker and saw my uniform on the floor. I wasn't sure what was going on, but I knew Luis was up to something. I looked over at him and he pretended not to see me. So I kept going, but by now I could feel the whole team looking at me. I didn't know what he had done to that uniform. All I knew was that I wasn't too anxious to grab it. And now I could hear guys beginning to laugh. Finally I reached down and moved the shirt. And there was this ugly damned fish, wearing my hat, grinning at me. Someone had stuck tongue depressors inside its mouth to make it look like it was smiling, but I didn't have to ask who that someone was. There was only one guy who'd do something like that. And of course he swore to God he didn't know a thing about it."

"Harper and me," Luis explains, "we're better than brothers."

One March evening in 1973 found the "brothers" barreling down the Interstate from St. Petersburg to Winter Haven following one of their typically unsuccessful visits to the dogs.

"You should see him at the track," Tommy laughs. "He's even funny there, just rooting for the dog that's got his money."

When you think of the modern athlete, especially one who starts for a prosperous franchise, you picture a heavy bankroll and the good life, but conversation in the car that night didn't sound anything like the casual banter of two guys who had it made.

"We'd go to the track and get busted," Tommy says. "It happened more than once. Then we'd get hungry on the long ride back. But as Luis would say, we'd just been 'killed by the dogs.' He'd look at me and I'd look back at him, and we'd just start roaring. Here we were, two major league ballplayers, starving, with about 90 cents between us! It just seemed funny, I guess. But there was this place in Lakeland that sold fried chicken and you could get three pieces for 79 cents. I can remember a few times when we couldn't even get up the 79 cents. So this night we count our money and find out we've just enough for those three pieces, but the place closes around eleven-thirty and we were still pretty far away. Luis starts to really move that car. I mean, he's going breakneck down the highway because we were really starving and we didn't want to miss that chicken. Then this damned red light starts flashing in the mirror, and a state trooper waves Luis over."

"Good evening, sir," the trooper began.

"How are you doing?" Tiant replied solicitously.

"You were going kind of fast across that bridge, weren't you?"

"Yeh," Luis nodded, quite seriously, "I was bringing in some heat!"

"The trooper just looked at him like he couldn't believe what he was hearing," Tommy reports. "Then he let us go. As we drove away I looked at Luis and said, ' "bringing in some heat?" Did you really say what I thought you said?' We laughed all the way to Lakeland."

The Sox had Tommy playing in center field one afternoon in Winter Haven and a high fly ball was hit his way. He properly tracked it down and then steadied his glove for the catch, but at the last instant he lost it in the sunlight. The ball smacked him on the right cheek, immediately raising a knot just below the eye.

Detroit's Norm Cash, who was jogging nearby, stopped and yelled over: "Hey, did that ball hit you on the head?"

"Yeah," Harper answered.

Cash dropped to his knees and began to laugh.

"I didn't mind that," Tommy says, "but I kept hearing this squeaky little familiar voice, way over by the clubhouse, screaming at me, trying to get my attention. I knew if I even looked like it might have hurt me Luis would have been all over me in the locker room. So I just tugged on my hat as if nothing had happened. But he kept yelling and screaming. So finally I turned to see what was going on, and there was Luis, rolling on the ground, laughing at me. He really got a big kick out of seeing that damned ball hit me on the head."

Tommy promised himself he'd get even. "But you don't get many chances to poke fun at Luis," he explains. "He doesn't hit, and usually he's not involved in many fielding plays."

But this time Tommy got lucky.

"He was pitching against Bill Freehan that afternoon," Harper recalls, "and he tried to fool him with one of those little sliders, only he didn't get it far enough outside. Bill hit a line drive right back at him, hitting him on the can. Luis picks up the ball and throws Freehan out to end the inning. Then he walks back to our dugout. He's got his head down because he *knows* I'm going to be looking at him. I came in and sat way down at the far end of the bench, but still Luis can *feel* me watching him. He keeps sitting there for a minute or so, waiting for me to say something. But I keep quiet. Finally he kind of casually peeks over at me and sees me staring at him and we both begin laughing at the same time. 'Man, where did that ball hit you?' I asked. Luis has tears in his eyes now, he's laughing so hard. 'On my ass,' he says. And I just rolled on the dugout floor.''

Harper was more than a friend to Luis; in some ways he was a security blanket, too, someone to confide in, to lean on and to count on.

Luis liked having Tommy around, which is how a warm-up routine got started.

"He's not superstitious or anything like that," Harper explains, "but he liked me to go out to the bullpen with him and hold a bat while he warmed up. It just became a habit. I started feeling funny about it when the crowds in Boston began giving him these big ovations as he left. We'd walk out that gate and I knew the cheers were going to start at any minute. It bothered me to be walking across the field with him, because I knew the cheers were for him, not me. It was like I didn't belong there. So it got to be a joke. We'd be walking side by side and all those people would be cheering like they already had the game won. 'I don't understand this,' I'd tell him. 'How can these people love *you?*' Luis would laugh like hell. Same thing when we got to the dugout. 'Do you hear that, Yaz?' I'd say. 'All that cheering for a broken-arm pitcher like him!' Then Yaz would get on him, too.

"But I'll tell you something about all that cheering. Luis saw the Boston fans boo Jim Plunkett and boo Yaz and boo Phil Esposito. We used to talk about it. The only two athletes we've never heard them boo are John Havlicek and Bobby Orr. Fans can be cruel in Boston just as much as in Philadelphia or any other city. When Luis first came up to the Sox and started losing, there was a group of fans in the bleachers who kept yelling unkind things at him whenever he warmed up. It really hurt him, although he never said a word about it publicly. But now the whole town was cheering and he loved every minute of it. In the back of his mind, though, I'm sure he realized it would stop the minute things went wrong. So he never let it go to his head."

Tiant's warning to Harper about never attempting to steal was not entirely in jest, for Luis never recognized a friend if he happened to be wearing a different uniform—not even Tommy.

"People see two friends playing against one another and automatically assume they're going to take it easy," Harper smiles, "but that simply isn't so. At least it isn't so with Luis.

"One year I was playing with Milwaukee and he was with the Twins. This was just before his injury. He got two quick strikes on me. He had been pitching me outside and he had me leaning. So now he winds up again and I'm still leaning out, looking for the slider. Instead, he throws me a fastball inside! There was no way I could even try to hit that thing, so I just took the pitch. And it was a beautiful strike. But the umpire called it a ball. Luis just about went crazy out there. He began screaming and hollering. In my own mind, of course, I *knew* I should have been walking back to the dugout. But I tried to look nonchalant, kicking the dirt and so on. Finally I gave him a disgusted look and said, 'Man, get back out there and pitch that ball!' Now he was really steaming. So he goes back and throws me a slider. He really fooled me with it. I hit practically one-handed *and the damned thing goes over the fence for a home run!* He gave me dirty looks all around the bases. It didn't make any difference to him if we had been friends for 100 years. He was angry.

"The next time up he knocked me on my ass with a fastball that hummed right over my coconut! It was a good one. He really put me flat on my back. I picked myself up and looked out at him and he was sort of grinning at me, like he was saying, 'Yeh, that's right, you're going down, too; you're no different than anybody else.'

"And I understood it.

"When I got back to the bench one of the guys said, 'Hey, I thought you two were buddies.'

"I told him we were, but once the game begins Luis can't tell me apart from the other eight batters. And that's the way it should be."

The Tiant-Harper escapades often involved a middleman named Yastrzemski.

"It's a funny thing about Yaz," Tommy says. "When new guys come to Boston they almost instinctively leave him alone. It's like they're afraid of him. But Carl really loves to kid around, and

Luis always brought out the best in him that way. Yaz would always instigate things. He'd always be egging Luis on. Or else he'd be encouraging me to pull something on Tiant. He'd say, 'Tommy, you gotta get him back!' I don't think most people realize what a fun type of guy Yaz is. But Luis would never play tricks on Carl as a rule because he always said Yaz *played hard*. That might mean he'd cut a leg off of your suit pants or something like that. Or maybe sneak over when Luis was reading a paper and swing a bat against the locker, scaring hell out of him. That's *playing hard*.

"Anyway, we had this thing going on the club for a while where you couldn't take a shower without getting a bucket of ice water thrown at you. Luis knew I couldn't stand that ice water. No way. I'd wait until everyone else was showered and dressed before I'd go in, just to make sure I wasn't caught. Then the fad seemed to die out and I wasn't really thinking about it anymore. So we play a night game in Boston and later on I'm walking into the shower room, minding my own business, and I see Luis standing there. Immediately, my mind tells me *watch out!* Then I see Yaz under a shower on the other side of the room and now I'm really beginning to wonder. But neither one of them had anything in his hands, and the gag had kind of died out, so I told myself I was probably safe. But just to be sure, I kept my hand on the faucet because that was another one of Tiant's little tricks: waiting until your eyes were covered with soap and then spinning the shower handle to cold.

"Luis kept talking to me all the time I showered. I forgot all about Yaz. But they had it all set up ahead of time. While Luis and I talked, Carl reached behind this wall in the room and grabbed the bucket of ice water."

By now half the team was congregated nearby, waiting to hear Harper howl.

"Hey, Tommy," Yastrzemski called.

Harper had just begun to turn when the frigid wave washed over him. It was at least a full minute before he could utter a word.

"I'll get you," he sputtered to Luis.

"Get him!" Luis protested, pointing toward Yastrzemski. "He did it. I didn't do anything."

"Yeh, but I'm going to get you, too, because I don't have to ask who set this up."

Like justice, Harper's revenge traveled with leaden feet. It took him nearly three months to repay Luis for the ice water incident, but he had to agree the wait was well worthwhile.

"Luis usually follows a set routine," Tommy explains. "Every day he'd come into the clubhouse, take off his clothes, wrap himself in a towel, and talk awhile. Then he'd grab a newspaper or magazine and head into the bathroom for a crap. Nobody ever paid any attention to this, until one day we heard him yell, 'Bye, Tommeee!' and then flush the toilet. "Of course it got a tremendous laugh. It got to be a habit. Day after day he'd go in there with his papers and pretty soon we'd hear that silly little voice going, *'Bye, Tommeee!'* and then the toilet would be flushed. You'd think after a while it would seem ridiculous, huh? But not the way Luis did it. He made it funnier every day, then he'd walk out and give me a foolish grin.

"I kept telling him I was really going to get him, but he just laughed. Actually it was almost impossible to get that guy. He was always on guard. When he was sitting on the john, for instance, he'd always keep peeking under the door, just to make sure no feet were moving around outside. There was no way you could sneak up on him."

Well, *almost* no way.

One day the Sox were playing in Yankee Stadium, and just before Luis put on his uniform he grabbed a copy of the New York *Times* and headed into the hopper. A few minutes later Yastrzemski—that little old middleman—rushed over to Harper's locker.

"Tommy," he whispered, pointing toward the bathroom, "he's not paying attention today."

Harper's face lit up as he went into action. A bucket was quickly secured from the trainer's room and filled to the brim with the coldest water in New York. Then Tommy tiptoed over to the bathroom entrance, followed by Yastrzemski, 23 players, and a coaching staff, all of whom tiptoed, too, forming a conga line of coconspirators.

A row of hand basins lined the wall opposite the entrances to the toilet stalls. Harper climbed on top of the end basin, balanced himself precariously, then reached for the bucket of water that Yastrzemski thoughtfully handed to him. Step by careful step Tommy inched along the row of basins until, at last, he was perched no more than three feet away from his unsuspecting pal.

Then he waited. The bucket was heavy and he was impatient, but it had taken weeks and weeks to arrive at this glorious moment. He wasn't going to rush things now. Finally he heard the shuffling of feet from behind the gray metal door, and then the familiar cry . . .

"Bye, Tommeee!"

Moments later a shivering Tiant emerged, looked up at the hysterical Harper and broke into a sheepish grin.

Justice—leaden feet and all—had prevailed.

Harper can tell Tiant stories for hours on end. So can Yastrzemski, Bill Lee, Stan Williams, Eddie Kasko, and others who have lived with Luis in locker rooms from Mexico City to Fenway Park.

"To most people, I suppose all of these things don't really seem funny," Tommy says. "But when you've got 25 guys together, day in and day out for seven months, you have to find ways to break the tension. And nobody ever found more ways to do that than Luis did. He's got to be the funniest man in baseball."

CHAPTER 22

The Man in White

"Every man who takes this job realizes he'll be fired some day," Eddie Kasko said upon his appointment to the Boston managerial post in 1970. "He's a fool if he doesn't. Your team must remain in contention or changes have to be made. It'll happen to me someday."

And it did, just before the conclusion of the 1973 season. His four-year record was 346–295, his teams finished second twice and third twice, and in each of his seasons Boston attendance hovered around the 1,500,000 mark.

But with the exception of that unbalanced '72 race, his Red Sox never seriously contended for the championship. As he predicted, it cost him his job.

"Maybe he was too nice a guy," Luis suggests. "I know he was very good to me, especially in the beginning when I was trying to make my comeback. Before he left I told him he'll always be my friend."

But Darrell Johnson, the new Red Sox manager in 1974, needed no introductions to Tiant. He had been the boss at Louisville when Pedro Ramos and José Santiago began to campaign for

Luis; he had been the instigator in getting Dick O'Connell's attention; and finally he had been the judge and jury that sent Tiant on his way to Fenway Park with a ringing endorsement.

Now he was going to have the pleasure of watching the polished result of those 1971 endeavors. But he'd have to wait awhile for, again in keeping with his established pattern, Luis' springtime record was as inconsistent as the weather in which he pitched.

He was chased in his first two starts, then lost an eight-strikeout, 2–1 decision to New York. He defeated Cleveland, 5–4, in a sloppy game and dropped his next two decisions to Texas and California for an overall record of 1–3 in April. His ERA for the month was 5.79.

He began May by yielding 10 hits to the Rangers for his third consecutive defeat, then came back four days later and shut out the Yankees on 86 pitches. In his next four starts that month he allowed 41 hits!

By the end of May he was 5–5, but warm weather was just around the corner, meaning the *real* Tiant was due to surface soon.

During his 2½ years in Boston, Luis had found many friends, and a handful of them would become very dear to him. That group included Felix Fernandez, of course. It also embraced Larry DeCelle, Director of Public Works for the town of Milton, Massachusetts, and his wife, Marta; Nick Trifone, a lifelong friend of Larry's and a probation officer at the Norfolk County Courthouse in Quincy, Massachusetts; and Robert (Buddy) Scheiber, a special justice of the Stoughton, Massachusetts, court.

"That group is like a family to Luis," Felix explains. "Some families you are born with and others you select. When you break with the past as Luis did, you have the gift of selection. Back in Cuba many friendships were formed because of political or social associations, but here we found a wide-open range of people. Luis and I came from an old past, an old background, and now it was like starting life all over. These new friends he met were very important to him."

From time to time in the years 1971–73 Maria would visit Luis in Boston, meeting those friends, attending games and—in private moments—discussing the future with Luis. The long periods of separation bothered her as much as they bothered Luis. The children needed a full-time father; she wanted a full-time husband; and Luis longed for a return to conventional family life, something he really hadn't known since boyhood. For a decade now his summers had been spent in Cleveland, Minnesota or Boston, and his winters had been spent in Nicaragua, Venezuela or Puerto Rico. There was no way Maria and the children could have followed that trail, so they remained at home in Mexico City while Luis pursued his career.

The 20–13 record in 1973, coming on the heels of his splendid performance down the 1972 homestretch, gave Luis a sense of permanency in Boston, a feeling of finally having found a major league home.

Now he wanted to make it a real home for Maria and the kids.

Maria was pregnant with their third child as the 1974 season began, and her doctor advised her not to leave Mexico City until after the baby was born early in July.

As soon as Luis arrived in Boston, following spring training, he began to think about buying a home.

"You can't do that until Maria gets here," Marta DeCelle advised him. "A woman should pick out her own home."

"I know what she likes," Luis maintained. "It's okay."

And so, between ball games and road trips, Luis began looking at real estate, usually accompanied by Larry or Nick. If he found something he thought would fit the bill, he'd have Marta visit it for a female appraisal.

At last he found what he was looking for, a home he felt was made for Maria, little Luis, Isabel and the baby on the way. It was a four-bedroom, contemporary trilevel ranch house, complete with a custom-built swimming pool, located on a lovely landscaped acre in Milton, abutting the exclusive Wollaston Country Club.

He arranged for the necessary papers to be drawn up, then had Marta take a series of photographs to be mailed to Maria, introducing her to her new home.

"Luis," Nick Trifone asked, "suppose she doesn't like it?"

"She will," he answered.

On June 1 Luis shut out the White Sox, 8–0, as Boston slipped into first place in the American League East. It was a neat five-hitter and the first time that Chicago had been held scoreless in 59 games. Yet he wasn't overpowering as he totaled only four strikeouts.

"I don't care if I don't strike out one batter," he explained to Peter Gammons of the *Globe*. "They can hit 27 fly balls, 27 grounders or 27 line drives. As long as they're 27 outs, I don't care. I'm getting older now. I have to save myself. I can still throw the fastball whenever I have to, but now I concentrate more on setting up the batters."

After a road win in Minnesota, hiking his record to 7–5, Luis returned to Fenway for an NBC Monday night game against the world champion Oakland A's in which he proceeded to demonstrate to the nation just what he had been trying to explain to Gammons.

He struck out seven and scattered six hits in registering his fourth consecutive triumph, 4–1, but it was his total command on the mound that had observers ooohing and aaahing all night.

"Did you see how he was bothering those hitters tonight?" NBC's Tony Kubek raved. "They were leaning and waiting, ready to pounce on his pitches, but he just held that ball in his glove and let them fidget."

"He was nasty tonight," Sal Bando agreed.

But Reggie Jackson had a better word for it.

"He was tricky," the Oakland slugger told writers. "That last time at bat he threw me five pitches: a fastball, a curve, a change-up, a slider and a knuckler. All of that in one time at bat! And every one of those pitches came in a good spot. That man is very tricky."

The guy with a bird's-eye view of Tiant's mastery was catcher Carlton Fisk, and he explained the secret of Luis' style quite succinctly to columnist Tim Horgan of the *Herald American*. "He always knows what he's doing, but the batter never does."

It had been a game with special meaning for Luis. The day before was Father's Day, and he had placed a call to Señor Tiant in Havana, who informed him he'd be listening to the game by radio.

In his next outing Luis worked 15 innings before dropping a 4–3 decision to the Angels. Nolan Ryan had lasted 13, during which he had 19 strikeouts.

Then he went 10 innings against the A's in Oakland and won, 2–1, with a three-hitter.

Back in Boston he completely baffled the Brewers, 9–0, as he struck out 10 and walked none, earning repeated ovations from the crowd of 26,562, including a thrilling standing tribute as he closed out the ninth.

"You know his fastball is his best pitch," Milwaukee's Johnny Briggs said, "but if you go up there looking for it he'll get you into trouble with his other stuff. He's really great."

Luis finished the month with a 12–2 romp over Cleveland, his ninth win in his last 11 starts. He was now 11–6.

His June record was 6–1, with a 1.22 ERA.

And the Red Sox were rolling right along with him. With the exception of one day, they had spent the entire month in first place and were leading by two as the schedule moved into July.

In October 1973, Luis made a personal religious commitment. There was never any fanfare or announcement, nor did he ever engage in any proselytizing, but for a period of one calendar year he wore nothing but white, including shoes, coats, hats, etc. The only exception to this dress code was the Red Sox uniform.

He refused to discuss the matter with teammates and writers, other than to tell them it was private and he wanted to keep it that way. Throughout the 1974 season he was rarely seen in public outside of the ball park. Bars, race tracks, restaurants and other places where crowds might congregate were generally considered off-limits; indeed, he even began eating his meals in his room on the road.

"The only time he really deviated from that routine was in the line of his job," a friend explained. "There was no drinking, no gambling, no public appearances. It wasn't any formal program or anything like that. Luis is a regular Roman Catholic. But he had selected this time in his life to devote one year to thanking God, or his Saint [Barbara], for all of the good things that had happened to him. You know, this is a very religious man, despite his reputation as a baseball comedian. There's a room in his house that few people ever see. It's almost like a little shrine or chapel. He's a very devout person, but he doesn't go around making a big thing out of it."

Like every other facet of his life, however, the white suit had its share of funny moments.

Bill Crowley, the Red Sox publicist, delights in relating the "tuxedo story," a typically Tiant anecdote. Crowley had contacted Luis down in Caracas during the winter of 1972–73, giving him instructions regarding the upcoming Boston baseball writers dinner, and he told him he'd be reimbursed for travel, meals and the rental of a tuxedo. When Luis arrived he handed Bill a receipt for the *purchase* of a tuxedo.

"You were supposed to rent one," Crowley complained.

"I tried to," Luis shrugged, "but I've got a funny build."

The next winter Crowley called him again. "This time," Bill remembers, "I figured I was all set. After all, he had the tuxedo we bought him the year before. So he pulls into town—*with no tuxedo*.

"Where's the one we bought you?" Crowley asked.

"It's no good," Luis explained. "I need a white one."

After a whirlwind tour of downtown Boston stores, an off-white formal suit was finally located.

"By the way," the exasperated Crowley inquired, "where is the other tuxedo anyway?"

"I gave it to my cousin," Luis smiled through cigar smoke.

The commitment to white clothing also brought about what Harper calls "the only time I ever saw Luis get *really* mad."

It was getaway day in Milwaukee, which usually means mild chaos as players scurry in and out of the showers while equipment men gather up uniforms, bats and paraphernalia, all of them mindful of the impending hour of departure.

In their haste the clubhouse boys apparently grabbed Tiant's white street socks and threw them into a bundle of dirty laundry.

"Who's got my socks?" Luis demanded.

No one answered.

"I want my socks," he repeated, becoming more agitated.

Still no response.

Harper, realizing Luis was in no mood for fooling, sidled over to Yastrzemski.

"Have you got them, Yaz?" he whispered.

"No," Carl said. "I thought you did."

By now the situation had reached crisis proportions.

"I'm not getting on that bus until I get my socks back," Luis warned, and he was adamant.

But eventually he was persuaded to accompany the team, though he was still fuming. He sat in an aisle seat, alone, and never spoke a word as the bus sped the squad to General Mitchell Field.

Meanwhile, in the back of the bus, Harper, Yaz and several other players began to giggle at the sight of the infuriated Tiant, sitting there in stone silence, all decked out in white from head to foot, with the exception of the bare ankles that rose out of his patent leather loafers.

"Orlando Cepeda began telling me things to yell to Luis in Spanish," Harper laughs. "I didn't know what I was saying, but it was *killing* Orlando! Pretty soon the whole team was getting into it, but Luis kept sitting there with no expression on his face."

At last Tommy left his seat and sauntered down the aisle. He started to walk past Luis, then stopped, looked down, reached out and lifted a white pant cuff. "Hmmm," he said, "nice socks you've got there, fella!"

With the rest of the team in hysteria, Tiant looked up at Tommy, who had tears in his eyes, and then had to relent.

"He ended up laughing harder than any of us," Tommy says. "But boy, was he mad at first."

The white wardrobe was really incidental, an outward manifestation of a very personal inner conviction.

He had always attended church, though not on a regular basis. "I don't go just for the sake of saying I went to church," he explains. "Some people go to show off a new $100 dress or $50 hat, but I don't think that's being fair to God or fair to the Church. We aren't supposed to be proudful people. When I go, I go to pray for my family, for my friends and for me."

In 1971, the year of great upheaval in his career, Luis joined a separate sect within the Church. It had branches throughout the United States and Mexico; his particular congregation was centered in New York.

"I don't want to say a lot about it," he explains. "The people who belong know all about the white and why I wore it. But outside we don't talk about it. I will tell you this. Some people may wonder if there is a God, but I don't. I believe He's upstairs. He's proved that to me. And I believe He's looking at every move we make. So many good things started happening to me. It was no accident. Like the way I came back when everybody was saying I was all through. God was good to me. I just wanted to pay Him a tribute. That's all."

CHAPTER 23

22 Wins and a Home

The Orioles routed Luis on July 4, getting 10 hits off him before Darrell Johnson yanked him in the seventh inning of a 10–6 defeat, but then he put together five consecutive complete game victories to hike his record to 16–7.

It had been an excellent month.

He beat Texas, 2–1, on a four-hitter, then shut out California with ease, 3–0. "He knows exactly what he wants to do on every pitch," Angels manager Dick Williams said. "What a tremendous competitor."

On July 19 Luis carried a no-hitter into the fifth against Texas, then yielded a run that ended his string of 21 consecutive scoreless innings. After the Rangers loaded the bases with one out in the ninth, he struck out Tom Grieve and Duke Sims to protect his 3–1 win.

Two days later, as he prepared to fly to Pittsburgh for the All-Star Game, he received a call from Mexico City. Maria had just given birth to their second son, named Daniel Alfredo Tiant. It was a double blessing for Luis, since the child's arrival meant the family would soon be reunited in that magnificent Milton home.

After bombing in the All-Star Game, 7–2 (the National League had now won 11 out of 12), in which he was charged with the loss, Luis won a pair of 5–4 victories over New York and Detroit to finish the month with a flourish.

The Red Sox, meanwhile, maintained their hold on first place.

By now a Tiant cult had formed at Fenway Park. The stirring ovations that had highlighted his past heroics now gave way to a daily love affair which saw the customers cheering Luis every time he appeared. Thousands of voices would join in a chant of "Loo-ie, Loo-ie" as the fans poured their affections upon him.

"They've simply adopted this guy," Bill Crowley says. "I can't pinpoint how it started or why. Who can define charisma? Ted [Williams] has a charisma that was almost unreal. He had this whole area by the ears. And in the early sixties [relief pitcher] Dick Radatz was the so-called Monster. This place used to get electrical when he walked out of the bullpen. But in the 19 years I've been associated with the Red Sox I've never seen anything like the way these fans love Luis."

Carl Yastrzemski had it that way for one Cinderella season, 1967, when he won the American League triple crown while leading the Sox to their "Impossible Dream" pennant. Talk about a Midas touch! Every move Carl made, at the plate or in the field, seemed to be choreographed for the ultimate emotional impact, even unto the last two days of the season when he batted seven-for-eight to personally lead the Sox into the Series. It might have been the finest individual season in baseball history; if not, it surely ranked among the very best. But then, once the great tide of euphoria passed, it became his personal albatross. Everything he ever accomplished in the future would inevitably be compared to 1967, which was both unrealistic and unfair. It had been a season to be savored, not repeated. But the world of sports, much like the real world outside, is caught up in what might be called the "what have you done for me lately?" syndrome. It's what made Roger Maris a "failure" for hitting 33 home runs in 1962, after his historic 61-homer performance the year before. There are some acts you just can't follow. And Yastrzemski surely had one in 1967.

So the greatest Red Sox player of the post-Williams era looked on with awe, and perhaps a tinge of longing, at the phenomenal relationship Luis enjoyed with the fans.

"This is Luis' place," he often observed. "He owns it. And he deserves it. Maybe it's impossible for a hitter to earn that kind of esteem because he's out there day after day and there's no way in the world he can deliver what the customers want every time. But it seems Luis is always at his best here. The people who come here know that when he is pitching they're going to see a hell of a show. Just his antics on the mound guarantee that. I think he's the most exciting athlete in baseball."

On August 4 at Shea Stadium (where the Yanks were playing during a two-year renovation of Yankee Stadium), Luis pitched his sixth consecutive complete game triumph. One of those exciting moments that Yaz alluded to came in the fourth inning when Boston held a 2–0 lead. New York had loaded the bases with one out, and Sandy Alomar was coming to bat.

"I had tipped off the men that I might bunt," Sandy later revealed, "just so they'd be ready for it. Luis threw me a fastball over the inside of the plate, right around the letters. When I popped it foul I didn't worry because it wasn't very high off the ground. Who was going to catch a ball like that?"

You guessed it.

As soon as the ball left Alomar's bat, Tiant began a mad dash for it. He raced over the first-base foul line, about 15 feet deep, and stabbed the ball with his outstretched glove, finally stumbling to a halt just beside the New York dugout.

"It was like chasing a sparrow," he chuckled later. "I kept running and the ball kept going."

"But why," Clif Keane of the *Globe* wanted to know, "were you even chasing it in the first place?"

"Because it wasn't a sparrow," Luis answered. "It was the ball. And those are the things you have to do to win a pennant."

The win gave him a 17–7 record, tops in the majors.

Milwaukee beat him, then Luis threw a four-hit shutout at the Angels for his eighteenth win, and he picked up No. 19 in a sloppy 9–6 contest with the Twins.

Then he had five days to rest before meeting the Oakland A's in Fenway Park where his bid for win No. 20 would be witnessed by a capacity crowd.

Maria had left her homeland often during her 14-year marriage to Luis, but always secure in the knowledge she'd be returning soon.

Now she was leaving for good, and she never felt so frightened, so unsure, so depressed in her life. She and Luis had often discussed the idea, but in the end the answer was always the same. Mexico City was home for her. Everything near and dear, everybody she cared about, was in that ancient city. And Luis always understood; indeed, with memories of Cuba haunting his mind, he could understand the trauma of leaving home better than most people would ever comprehend. So, with only occasional proddings, the issue remained dormant for years. But now that the children were growing older, needing their father more than ever, she realized that the choice had come down to Mexico City or a happy home. And that, of course, was no choice at all. So she told Luis to go ahead and find a home, and that she would follow once the baby arrived.

On Thursday night, August 22, she watched as her brother Rafael and little Mario Villiseñor, one of Luis' best friends, gathered all of her belongings from the apartment and packed them into Rafael's car for the trip to Central Airport. Mario was going to accompany her and the children to Boston. That would make the trip easier. But nothing could soothe the anguish she felt as she stood at the foot of the runway while Rafael kissed the children goodbye, then turned to bid her a loving farewell. She had never known such a feeling of emptiness. As the plane flew off into the night she closed her eyes and cried.

Friday afternoon, a couple of hours before he was due to leave for Fenway Park, Luis reached for a phone.

"Nicky, I need three things. I want a pool table like the one you've got in your playroom. And I need a television set. And I need some telephones in the house."

Nick Trifone shook his head as he sat in his office at the Norfolk County Courthouse.

"He wanted it all done that day," he remembers. "It's Friday afternoon! Maria's plane is due in at six-thirty, and Luis is due to begin pitching at seven-thirty. But here he is, running around getting all the last details set for when the wife, the two kids and the brand-new baby walk into the home that night. Well, we got the television set with no problem, and I found a local vendor who agreed to deliver the pool table on his last stop of the day. But the telephone company! You know what it's like dealing with them. Anyway, we managed to get the phones in, too. And now Luis was finally relaxed. This was going to be the fulfillment of a dream. That night, right at seven-thirty, I'm sitting in Fenway Park and out waltzes Tiant. And I'll never forget thinking how cool the guy was, like he had nothing on his mind at all."

The plane, meanwhile, was late, due to a delayed changeover in Chicago. Mario was fidgeting in his seat, looking at his watch and grumbling: "We won't get there until the seventh inning!" The plans called for him and little Luis to immediately take a cab to Fenway Park while Marta DeCelle drove Maria, Isabel and baby Danny to the home in Milton.

"I remember when the door on the plane opened," Marta smiles. "Mario just dropped everything he was carrying, grabbed Luis' arm and took off for the game. I felt so bad for Maria. She is a very attractive woman, but this night she looked so tired. Don't forget, she had just had the baby a few weeks earlier. Then she had to pack everything for the trip. And now she was just getting off of a very long flight. It was a difficult time for her."

As soon as the 35,866 fans spotted Luis walking out of the bull-pen with Harper, following their traditional warm-up routine, the roar that swept across Fenway was thunderous. The whistles and cheers and shouts of encouragement didn't begin to abate until he disappeared into the Red Sox dugout. Tiant had won 17 of his last 19 decisions, including 15 complete games and four shutouts. No other pitcher in the majors could match those figures.

When Harper, batting leadoff, drove Vida Blue's third pitch over the left-field wall for a quick 1–0 lead, the ball park was a bedlam. Everyone *knew* that's all Tiant would need. But the Athletics, once again leading the American League West and intent upon winning their third consecutive world championship, were not intimidated by anyone, including Tiant. In six of the first seven innings they got their lead batter on base, but Luis kept managing to escape. His biggest threat had come in the third, when Bill North led off with a double down the left-field line. Tiant fired three pitches past Bert Campaneris for one out. Then he struck out Reggie Jackson on a fastball Reggie's still never seen. And finally, twisting a full 90 degrees before releasing the ball, he got Sal Bando on a weak fly to center. The threat had died, one-two-three, and cries of "Loo-ie, Loo-ie" filled the night air.

By the time Mario and young Luis arrived in the bottom of the eighth, it was no longer a contest. The Red Sox wound up with a 3–0 victory, fattening their American League East lead to seven full games, and Luis wound up with his twentieth victory, making him the first Boston pitcher to post back-to-back 20-win seasons since Dave Ferriss did it in 1945 and 1946.

"There is no shame in losing to that man," a gracious Jackson told reporters. "We were beaten by a very great pitcher tonight. He's the best in the league right now."

On the other side of the city, a car was just emerging from the Sumner Tunnel, one of two parallel tubes running beneath Boston Harbor that connect East Boston (and Logan International Airport) to the mainland. The radio static suddenly cleared, and the two women could hear announcer Ned Martin shouting over the roar of the crowd.

Maria looked down at baby Danny and whispered: *"Su papa gano."* (Your father won.)

After showing Maria through the house, Marta took Isabel with her as she left to pick up her own children. Maria sat in a chair in the downstairs game room, holding the baby, alone for the first time since leaving the apartment in Mexico City.

"It felt so strange," she recalls. "It didn't feel like it was my house. When Marta returned with the children later I was still sitting in the same place."

Within an hour, however, the home was bustling with activity as friends began arriving for a combination postgame and welcome-home party that lasted into the wee stages of the following morning.

"There was even a group from the Latin-American press there interviewing Luis," Marta remembers. "People were all over the house. And all I could think of was how nice it would be when everybody left and allowed that poor woman to get some rest."

The Sox and Luis were sitting on top of the world following that dramatic win over Oakland. Baltimore and New York were tied for second at seven games back, which was tantamount to saying the Sox had the divisional title in their back pockets. And Luis, with 20 wins on August 23, had another six or eight starts remaining. The Cy Young Award seemed practically assured.

But, like the best-laid plans of mice and men . . .

The club had received a severe jolt on June 28 when Pudge Fisk, hitting .299 with 11 homers, sustained severe ligament damage in his left knee while blocking the plate in the final inning of a 2–1 loss at Cleveland. The injury sidelined him for the rest of the season, but even without his potent bat—and excellent defense—the Sox had continued to win.

Now, suddenly, they fell into an irreversible tailspin brought on by a batting slump that made the 1968 Indians look like Murderers Row. Day by day the Boston lead eroded as both the Orioles and Yankees came to life.

The Sox lost five of their remaining seven games in August, then kicked off September by dropping six in a row (for an eight-game losing streak).

Beginning August 20, the Yankees won 11 out of 12.

Starting August 29, the Orioles won 10 in a row.

On September 4 the Yankees shut out Milwaukee and moved into a first-place tie with the Red Sox, who were losing their *third consecutive shutout* down in Baltimore! The Orioles were now two games back.

A day later the idle Yanks took sole possession of the lead when the Sox were beaten by the Brewers.

All the joy and lightness had left the Boston locker room. Not only were the Sox no longer leading, it was painfully obvious they were no longer even *contending,* even though the standings showed them right in the thick of the race.

"Yet we weren't playing bad ball," Darrell Johnson insists. "If we had been out there booting plays and making mental errors it would have been a different story. But we were actually playing good ball in the field, maybe the best we'd played all year long. We just couldn't buy a damned hit when we needed one."

Indeed, in the month of September the team batting average was .203.

The slow demise was tortuous, especially to the older players.

"I've been in the majors 12 years now," Harper said, "and I'm still waiting to get into my first World Series. I'm not sure the young kids here can really appreciate what that means yet. They've still got a lot of chances left. But the older you get, the more you realize your opportunities are slipping away. I may never get this close to a championship again. Guys who've played in the Series tell me there's no other feeling in the world quite like it. Maybe if you had a great career like Ernie Banks did it would compensate for never winning a championship. But my career would certainly never compensate that way. I just have to get into at least one World Series before my playing days are over."

Nothing personified Boston's power failure more clearly than Tiant's next four outings after that twentieth win against Oakland.

He went to Chicago and lost, 3–0.

Then the Red Sox went on to Baltimore, where he worked the opener of a doubleheader, striking out eight, scattering three hits, and losing, 1–0. Bill Lee lost the nightcap by a 1–0 score, too.

Four days later the Brewers came to town and Luis lost again, 2–0.

His frustration reached a peak in his next appearance, against New York. Luis and Pat Dobson were hooked up in a marvelous duel before 33,174 fans at Fenway. Going into the ninth, Boston held a 1–0 lead (an unearned run, of course). With one out, Lou Piniella drew a walk after fouling off three consecutive three-and-two pitches and fleet Larry Murray was sent in to run for him. Chris Chambliss followed with a line drive into the right-field corner, and soon all hell broke loose. Dwight Evans casually retrieved the ball as Murray crossed the plate and Chambliss pulled into third. The Sox followed the ball's flight and were sure an infraction had taken place, but when it became obvious that no ruling was forthcoming, both Evans and Darrell Johnson charged first base umpire Hank Morgenweck, claiming the ball had struck a fan who then dropped it back onto the playing surface for a

ground-rule double. After a hurried conference, crew chief Marty
Springstead ordered Chambliss back to second, infuriating the
New Yorkers, and allowed Murray's tying run to stand, which
sent Johnson into such a rage he was promptly ejected.

"I thought the fan reached over the wall and touched the ball,"
Springstead later explained. "That would make it spectator interference, which is different than a ground-rule double that actually
lands in the stands. Spectator interference allows the umpire to
decide where the runners *would have* ended up if the interference
had not occurred."

All of this didn't help Tiant, who left the game with no decision
after nine superb innings. At that point the Red Sox had given
Luis the grant total of *one unearned run in 38 innings!* In that
span he had lost three consecutive games in which Boston was
shut out, and then worked nine more innings with nothing to
show. But he never blew his top.

"I thank God that He gave me the ability to control my mind,"
he said. "Sometimes things go wrong even when you're doing your
best. That just shows none of us is perfect. So I keep trying with
all my heart, and if that's not good enough, I'm not going to hang
my head and go crazy. I'll just go back out next time and try
again. As long as I know we're all trying our best, there's no way
I'm going to criticize anyone."

It was a graciousness that didn't go unnoticed.

"Once in a great while he loses his temper," Larry Claflin wrote
of Luis in the *Herald American*. "Last year he refused to talk to
the press after one particularly tough loss. Ordinarily, however, he
keeps his feelings to himself. If he is bitter, he hides it. The Red
Sox have had some monumental tempers on the mound in past
years. Lefty Grove used to smash things with bats when he lost a
tough game. Wes Ferrell used to stamp on his own wristwatch.
Tiant lights a cigar and goes home."

The Sox continued to sink in the standings. They were now in
second place, tied with the Yankees, two games behind the very
hot Orioles.

On September 15 Luis pitched his first bad game in a month,
getting clobbered by Milwaukee. Then, in his sixth attempt at his
twenty-first win, he pitched a five-hitter against Detroit and lost,
3–1.

His drought ended on September 24 in Shea Stadium when he shut out the Yankees, 4–0, before 46,448 infuriated fans who showered the field with tennis balls, beer and trash. The win, Tiant's seventh shutout (tops in the majors), coupled with Roger Moret's 4–2 victory in the nightcap, pulled the Yankees out of the first-place tie they shared with Baltimore.

In his final appearance of the season, Luis fired a three-hitter at the Tigers and won his twenty-second game, 7–2.

His record on August 23 had been 20–8.

It ended up 22–13.

And Jim (Catfish) Hunter ended up with the Cy Young Award after posting a 25–12 record for Oakland.

More important to Luis, however, the Orioles ended up winning the American League East after scoring 28 victories in their final 34 games!

New York was second, two games back.

And Boston was third, seven games out of the running.

It was time to go home. To Milton.

CHAPTER 24

One Man's Castle

Nothing that could have happened in that 1974 season—not the Cy Young Award, not even the pennant—could have meant more to Luis than that home in Milton; not *that* particular house, but rather the overall concept of a family home where father, mother and children shared the security and sense of permanence that are too often taken for granted in the mobile society we live in today.

Quae est domestica sede incundior?

Indeed, as Cicero pondered a century before the birth of Christ, "What is more agreeable than one's home?"

For Luis Tiant, the answer was *nothing*. The whole idea of seeing the kids off to school each morning; of driving from the ball park to his backyard; of celebrating birthdays, anniversaries and holidays; of sharing in the day-to-day joys and sorrows of the woman he married and the children they reared: for Luis, these were the real things of value, and all of the other triumphs were merely transitory pleasures to be enjoyed while they lasted and then forever stored in the mists of nostalgia.

Home, according to puckish Robert Frost, was simply the place, "where, when you go there, they have to take you in."

But in Luis' mind it was nothing less than the proverbial castle.

"It was like watching a kid with a toy," Larry DeCelle smiles. "He was out in that yard all the time, puttering around with the pool, the lawn, the shrubs, anything at all. He loved the place. Once he asked if he could borrow a couple of saws to trim some bushes. He got so carried away I had to stop him before he cut down everything in sight. I told him, 'Luis, you stick to pitching and leave the gardening to somebody else.' "

Those first few months together in Milton should have been among the happiest times of all for Luis and Maria. Instead, they were filled with uncertainty and, for Maria, unhappiness.

"Sometimes I'd just sit there and cry and cry all day," she said. "And Luis would get mad at me."

At least it seemed that way back then, but in retrospect she understands the anguish he experienced in those months as well.

"I felt so bad for her," he remembers. "I knew she was homesick for her country, her family and her friends. I could understand that because I had felt the same way, too, when I was told I couldn't go back to Cuba. It's not easy when you don't speak good English and you don't know many people. In Mexico everybody talks to everybody else. But up here people keep to themselves more, and that's harder on a woman. I knew why she was unhappy."

But life is funny in the way it uses hardship to bring people closer together. Luis and Maria, faced with perhaps the biggest dilemma of their marriage, talked and talked and talked, weighing every aspect of the move they had made, a move that could always be rescinded by simply driving a "For Sale" into the manicured front lawn and then placing a call to the ticket office at Logan International Airport. There was always that escape valve.

It would have meant a return to their old divided existence, however, and Maria didn't want that.

So they continued to talk it out.

"We bought this house so that I could be with you," Luis said. "And with the kids. I want to be able to help you with them."

She began to cry again.

"What have I done wrong?" he asked.

She shook her head. "Nothing."

"Then why are you crying?"

"Maybe I'll never be able to go home again."

"You will," he promised. "And if the kids want to go back someday, they can, too. But I'm making my money here, so we should be living here. Besides, we want the kids to get a good education. We want them to go to American schools and learn English, just like we did. We have to be thinking of that. We've got a chance to make a good life for them. You have to look at it that way."

In the end, she realized, he was right.

And time began to heal her wounds.

"I love her," Luis says. "I'll love her until I die. She's so good to the kids. I know that's the way mothers are supposed to be, but a lot of them aren't. And she's been so good to me, too. Whatever I've got today, I've got because of her. She's been with me right from the beginning. So it killed me to see her unhappy. I just thank God everything worked out okay."

Marta DeCelle, who speaks excellent Spanish, spent hours with Maria and the children, helping to prepare them for their first day at school.

"It was funny," Marta says. "I spent a week making sure Isabel knew how to say, 'Where's the bathroom?,' just so she wouldn't get stuck. But after a couple of days at school she was coming home sprouting all kinds of English. Maria and I just looked at each other and laughed, as if to say, 'What were we worried about?' "

Still, Luis was leaving nothing to chance.

"He asked me to go with him to PTA meetings in the beginning," Marta remembers, "just to be sure the children were getting proper help because of the language barrier. He wanted to know everything about the classes they were taking and how well they were doing. He's really a wonderful father."

But he was also a baseball superstar in a city that is absolutely in love with the game. That was a handsome state of affairs, of course, as long as it was kept in perspective. Luis had learned how to handle fame. He had learned, in Kipling's immortal words, ". . . to meet with Triumph and Disaster and treat those two imposters just the same; to talk with crowds and keep his virtue; to walk with Kings, and not lose the common touch." Modern kids would say "his head was screwed on right." But he knew only too well that fame could hurt a child as badly as a man, maybe even more so. That's why he called young Luis aside for a father-son talk on the eve of the first day of school.

"Don't ever let other kids bother you about who I am," he counseled. "You have to make your own life. You can't ever think that being Luis Tiant's son will get you anything you want, because that just isn't so. You've got to do things for yourself. All I can give you is a good home, a good education and my love. Everything else is up to you. Don't ever forget that."

The winter of 1974–75 was a happy one for Luis. He had decided against playing winter ball, correctly surmising that a 34-year-old arm needed rest after pitching 312 innings. Besides, the kids were still getting oriented to their new surroundings, just as Maria was, and he wanted to make the transition as smooth and pleasant as possible.

With friends always stopping by, and buddies like Felix and Harper living a few miles away, home was really *home* again, just the way he remembered it from those unforgotten days in Nicanor del Campo.

He had climbed to the summit of his profession, and now he had surrounded himself with the kind of private life he always dreamed of.

What more could any man want or expect?

But there was something else, and it never stopped troubling him, not even in the happiest of times.

He talked about it one day that December, just as Christmas drew nigh.

"My father is going to be 70 years old soon, and I don't know how many years he has left. It's been almost 15 years now since I saw him. I don't say much about it, except to certain friends. There's no point in complaining. But 15 years is a long time. I think I've paid enough. I think my mother and father have paid enough, too. He's working down there at a garage, serving gas, and I can't even send him a dime for a cup of coffee on Christmas. I can't do anything to help him. We've lost so much time already. I'd like to make the rest of their lives as nice as possible, but politics says I can't do that. I have nothing to do with politics. I never did. And neither did my parents. I don't see why they should have to pay for politics all these years. There's no question this is the best country in the world. America has been very good to me. But I miss Cuba, and I miss my parents. And what really hurts is that they're only 90 miles away from the United States. Maybe if they were half a world away things might seem different. But 90 miles. I could almost walk that far. And I would—I would run—if I could see them again."

Still, Luis was inclined to count his blessings that holiday season.

And he had many of them.

CHAPTER 25

A Letter to Castro

Luis knew what a winter of idleness would mean when spring training rolled around; all of those past March bouts with adhesions, shoulder stiffness and muscle pulls had taught him well the importance of reporting in good condition. So one morning, a week or so before he was due to fly to Winter Haven for the opening of the 1975 camp, he accompanied Judge Buddy Scheiber to the Brockton, Massachusetts, YMCA for a session of jogging.

Scheiber was one of those friends close enough to have talked with Luis about his parents' situation. Buddy knew the depths of Tiant's sadness, and the utter needlessness of the separation had bothered him all winter long. The more he thought about it, the more he felt compelled to intervene. Most likely it would be a futile gesture, but at least Luis would know that he tried. He had been an assistant attorney general under Edward W. Brooke back in the early sixties when the junior senator from Massachusetts had held the attorney general's office in Massachusetts, and though their paths divided when Brooke moved on to Washington in 1966, Scheiber had nevertheless maintained a close relationship with his former boss.

"I don't know how much good this might do," Buddy told Luis

that morning as they sat in the locker room, "but I could ask the senator to look into the situation."

"Okay," Luis replied noncommittally.

"He [Luis] didn't seem too excited by the idea," Scheiber remembers. "Luis is pretty much of a realist. He sits back and listens, and when things happen—that's when he believes them. It's not that he didn't believe I was seriously interested, or that other friends were interested; it's just that he didn't want to raise any false hopes. And I couldn't blame him."

Later that day Scheiber placed a call to recently retired Dorchester District Court officer Bill Jackson, one of Brooke's confidants, and asked him to pass the word along to the senator. Within a matter of days Brooke's office notified Scheiber that Tiant's situation would be reviewed for possible action.

"Now all we can do is wait," Buddy advised.

Luis nodded. He had learned how to wait a long time ago.

From a personal point of view Luis found 1975 a year of coming and going: Stan Williams, his buddy and benefactor in Cleveland and Minnesota, was coming to be Darrell Johnson's new pitching coach; and Tommy Harper, old "alligator breath" himself, was going to the California Angels in exchange for utility infielder Bob Heise.

"Nobody in Boston knew me at all," the good-natured Heise said later that season. "My wife and I would go someplace and I'd be introduced as a Red Sox player, but nobody would recognize me. Then someone would explain I was the guy they got for Tommy, and inevitably the response would be, 'Oh, yeh, we really liked Tommy a lot!' That would have been depressing except that I knew what a great guy he was. So I understood it."

It was also the year that Hank Aaron was coming to the American League, bringing the all-time record of 733 home runs with him to Milwaukee. The Brewers were scheduled to open their season in Boston, and a boisterous crowd of 34,019 jammed Fenway in 52-degree weather to watch Hammerin' Hank face El Tiante, as the local press enjoyed calling Luis.

An hour or so prior to game time, as the Sox relaxed in their clubhouse following batting practice, the irrepressible Tiant ambled over to Yastrzemski's locker and began throwing Carl's street clothes onto the carpeted floor.

"A million-dollar star wearing cheap shirts!" he yelled. "Look at this coat. How old is it? Five years?"

The coat was just about to join the disheveled shirts when Yaz came running to its rescue while the rest of the squad looked on and laughed.

"Do you believe that guy?" newcomer Tim McCarver grinned to a reporter. "That's our Opening Day pitcher. You can see how much the tension bothers him, can't you?"

Luis went the route and beat the Brewers, 5–2, holding Aaron to one walk. At one point late in the game Milwaukee threatened Boston's lead, but Tiant quickly extinguished the rally by retiring Aaron and George Scott on *two* pitches.

After splitting a pair of appearances against the Orioles, home and away, Luis lost a masterpiece in Detroit, 1–0. After retiring the first 14 batters in a row, all of whom were waving harmlessly at his deliveries, he tossed a changeup to rookie Danny Meyer, and the young Tiger swatted it into the chummy right-field seats. With Mickey Lolich on target, setting down the final 15 Boston batters, the lone run was sufficient to offset Tiant's two-hitter.

"I never saw anything like him before," Meyer said. "So I just went up there swinging, hoping to get my bat on the ball."

Five days later Cleveland routed Luis, 8–1, giving him a 2–3 record for the month of April.

Before heading out for the fifth inning of that game, Tiant turned to Darrell Johnson and told him, "You'd better watch me, because it's starting to go."

He was talking about his strength and, subsequently, his effectiveness.

"The biggest percentage of pitchers just flat don't want to come out of a game, period," Johnson noted. "But Luis will always tell you when he's starting to slip, when he's beginning to tire, because he's always thinking about winning as a team rather than as an individual. That's just one more quality I admire in the man."

On May 1 a news story broke, temporarily overshadowing everything else—including baseball—in Luis' life.

Senator George McGovern was about to leave for Cuba where

he planned to visit with Fidel Castro. Though the trip was unofficial, meaning McGovern had no authorization to enter into negotiations with Castro, he nevertheless intended to explore the possibilities of reopening diplomatic relations between the two countries. If America could carry on relations with Peking and Moscow, McGovern maintained, there was no reason for continuing a closed-door policy toward Havana.

When Senator Brooke learned of his colleague's upcoming trip, he asked him if he'd be willing to personally convey a message to Castro. McGovern said yes, and the following letter was prepared:

United States Senate
Washington, D.C.

Edward W. Brooke
Massachusetts

May 2, 1975

Prime Minister Fidel Castro
Republic of Cuba
Havana, Cuba

Mr. Prime Minister:

I am hopeful that Senator McGovern's visit to your country will prove beneficial to the efforts to normalize relations between our countries. While achievement of normalization will be difficult, it is an objective that merits the attention of both our governments.

My specific interest in writing to you is to seek your assistance on a matter of deep concern to myself and one of my constituents, Mr. Luis Tiant. I am sure you know of Luis as a star pitcher for the Boston Red Sox.

Luis's parents, Luis Eleuterio Tiant and Isabel Rovina Vega Tiant, reside at Calle 30 3312, Apt. 9, Mariano, Havana, Cuba. He has not had the chance to spend any significant time with them for many years. Naturally, he has a great desire to do so.

Luis's career as a major league pitcher is in its latter years. It is impossible to predict how much longer he will be able to pitch. Therefore, he is hopeful that his parents will be able to visit him in Boston during this current baseball season to see their son perform. I am sure we both agree that this is a reasonable desire.

I have contacted the State Department and have been assured that the granting of visas to enter the United States will be no problem. Therefore, with your help, I am confident that a reunion of Luis and his parents is possible this summer. Such a reunion would be a significant indication that better understanding between our peoples is achievable.

I look forward to receiving your response.

Sincerely,
Edward W. Brooke

McGovern arrived in Havana on Monday, May 5, and was not scheduled to meet with Castro until Thursday, the day of his departure.

On Tuesday night he was the dinner guest of Carlos Rafael Rodriguez, the Vice Prime Minister of Cuba. The leisurely meal lasted until almost 11 P.M. as McGovern exchanged light and casual banter with Rodriguez. Suddenly word was received that Castro had just arrived and was waiting to meet the senator in an adjacent living room.

"I was a bit startled to hear that," McGovern remembers, "because I hadn't expected to see him for two more nights."

Moreover, McGovern was also a bit apprehensive.

"I really didn't know what to expect," he explains. "But he was a perfect host. He's a rather compelling figure, yet, curiously enough, he speaks softly and in a cultured manner. But he's a man who conveys great physical strength. I would describe him as a charismatic, appealing figure."

Castro had just attended a national playoff game between Havana and Oriente, his home province and the birthplace of his revolution. Oriente lost.

"He was a bit down about that," McGovern recalls, "but we spent an hour talking that night. He had a great admiration for young men who have participated in battle, so he raised some questions about my war record, and we talked about my days as a bomber pilot. It was obvious he had read up on me and knew quite a bit about me. He asked about the 1972 presidential campaign, and told me if he had been an American he would have voted for me. It was a friendly kind of conversation."

But McGovern had the feeling that Castro was, in effect, sizing him up. Plans were made for the two men to meet again the following night, at which time McGovern would get down to the issues at hand. This initial meeting had been strictly an impromptu get-together and, therefore, was not the proper setting for serious discussions.

"I didn't want to get into the main agenda right then," McGovern says. "It was obvious this visit had been sort of an ice-breaker for him. But I thought it might be a good idea to begin our association with a human-interest angle. I knew he was a baseball fan, and I thought the timing was right because he had just come from the national championship games. So I brought up the Tiant matter that night."

His reaction?

"I think he was kind of intrigued by it. He knew all about Tiant, of course."

Then McGovern handed him the letter from Brooke. Castro studied it pensively, as if he were playing it over in his mind.

"Well," he finally responded, "I think that can be done. But let me check on it and I will give you the answer when we meet tomorrow."

The following afternoon McGovern sat down across a table from the khaki-clad ruler to begin an exchange that would last from 4:30 P.M. until 3:00 A.M. on Thursday.

"I've checked on your request about Mr. Tiant's parents," Castro said, opening the discussion, "and they've been advised that they can go to Boston and stay as long as they wish."

CHAPTER 26

Shoulder, Back or Old Age?

On Thursday evening, May 8, a reporter called Tiant's room at the Hotel Grand in Anaheim where the Red Sox were to begin a three-game series the next night. Luis, of course, had already received the news, and he no doubt expected the rash of calls that were to follow, but he was visibly upset by all inquiries from the media. He preferred to keep the lowest possible profile, lest any waves be created that might jeopardize the agreement.

"I pray I'll see them again," he said in his only public statement, "and when I do it will be the greatest day of my life."

With that, he returned his attention to baseball.

Two days later he pitched a four-hitter against the Angels, retiring the first 15 batters he faced, and he lost, 2–0. A year earlier a mild *cause célèbre* erupted when California manager Bobby Winkles told reporters that Tiant was a "junk man." Luis took the heat. "You tell him I pitch better than he manages," he snapped to one writer. Harper and Yastrzemski, of course, thought the entire incident was delightful and kept teasing Luis about his "junk." Now Tommy was playing for the Angels, and late in the game he drew a base on balls.

"Watch this," he winked to first-baseman Yastrzemski. "Hey,

you know something? It's true. You *do* throw junk!" he yelled over to the pitcher's mound. "Come on, throw some more of that junk! Is that the best you can do?"

If looks could kill, he'd have been called the *late* Tommy Harper.

In his next outing the Sox again failed to give Luis any support at all as he lost to Kansas City, 3–0, his fifth loss in eight decisions, and the third time the team was shut out behind him.

His record climbed to 4–5 when the Sox did a number on Oakland, 10–5, and then he reached the .500 mark when Harper's Angels returned to Fenway Park, where Luis beat them, 6–1, helped immeasurably by four Boston home runs, including a 440-foot blast by Yastrzemski.

Tiant would have had a shutout, except for a blooper pitch he threw to Tommy with Mickey Rivers on first. The ball came in high, and Harper poked it off the left-field wall as Rivers raced all the way home.

"Was he ever mad!" Tommy laughs. "He spun around and fired a pickoff throw right at me on second base. I ducked just in time. He really wasn't trying to hit me. He just wanted to let me know he was thinking about it because I had cost him his shutout."

The next day, Saturday, saw the Sox romp again, 6–0. It also saw Luis extract a full measure of revenge for Tommy's "junk ball" tirade.

It began when Harper, standing by the batting cage, looked over into the Boston dugout where Tiant, wearing a Donald Duck mask, danced and yelled out "Liver Lips!," one of his pet names for Tommy.

But the worst was yet to come.

"Winkles decided to try me at first base," Tommy said. "I had played only about eight games there before we pulled into Boston, but I hadn't missed a ball or made an error or done anything bad yet. So that's where I'm playing Saturday for the first time in Boston. Well, don't you know, the very first batter is Cecil Cooper, and he hits a ground ball right at me. And you know what happened next. The damned ball hit the heel of my glove, bounced up, hit me on the chest, then hit me on the chin! As soon as it landed on the ground, I reached for it, but it started rolling away. And when I went to chase it, my foot kicked it halfway to second base.

"Out of the corner of my eye I can see Luis. He's laying down on the top step of the dugout, just hysterical. I'm trying not to look over there. Cooper tells me, 'He's all over you!,' and I just nod back at him, but I'm still not looking. Meanwhile, Luis is yelling and screaming to get my attention, and I can hear a lot of laughing going on. So finally I peek over there.

"He's waving his arms at me, and I just can't believe what I see. He had a chest protector on, and shin guards, and a mask, *and gloves taped onto both of his shoes!*

"And he's yelling, 'Take these, you need them!'

"Nobody else in the world would think of something like that."

Boston was leading the division when June got under way, and all of baseball was raving about two spectacular Red Sox rookies —Freddy Lynn and Jim Rice—who were taking American League pitchers by storm. Both homered to help Luis nail down a woolly 11–9 win over the Twins on June 1; then the third youthful member of that dynamic outfield trio, 23-year-old Dwight Evans, hit two homers (including a grand slam) to power Tiant past the Twins again five days later in Boston, 13–10!

Following a bad showing against Texas, Luis beat the Royals, 4–3, aided by Lynn's three-run homer and Rice's game-winning sacrifice fly. Then he threw a three-hitter at the Tigers, which was completely overshadowed by a fabulous Lynn performance: three home runs, a triple (which missed being a homer by a foot) and a single, good for 10 RBI! Boston won, 15–1, and Luis had a 9–6 record.

Four days later he struck out a dozen Orioles in a 5–1 victory, ending an excellent 9–4 road trip for the Sox, who continued to set the pace in the American League East.

On June 26 a crowd of 34,293 packed Fenway to watch Luis battle the Yankees, who had put together a hot streak and taken a 1½-game lead over Boston. And Luis gave them a vintage performance, striking out eight New Yorkers with a full array of twists, spins and pirouettes that had the visitors wide-eyed. He won easily, 6–1, giving him seven consecutive victories over the Yankees in Fenway Park. And the overflowing stands reverberated with cries of "Loo-ie, Loo-ie!"

"It's like going to a concert or listening to the opera," Bill Lee once said to Clif Keane of the *Globe*. "The orchestra comes out and everything starts banging and it shakes the place. Then it comes to the middle part of the symphony and things get very calm and sweet, and you want to kind of fall asleep. Then, all of a sudden, you sense that the end is coming. Everyone starts getting noisy again. The whole gang is letting out with all the instruments. Then, boom! The whole show is over. That's Tiant! Hard at the start, a little sweet, slow stuff in the middle, and then the big explosion at the end."

By the end of June Luis had an 11–7 record, including eight wins in his last 10 decisions, and the Red Sox had a one-game lead in the standings. For the third time in four years Red Sox fans were thinking pennant, and though history had taught them to be wary of midseason mirages, it was becoming increasingly difficult to resist jumping aboard the Boston bandwagon. In addition to Lynn, Rice and Evans in the outfield, the Sox had superb young talent at shortstop (Rick Burleson) and behind the plate (Fisk), plus proven veteran talent along the bases in Yaz (first), recently acquired Denny Doyle and/or Doug Griffin (second) and Rico Petrocelli (third) There were no mirrors needed this time, nor was there an "Impossible" label on the dream.

The Red Sox were for real.

But Tiant, the workhorse who traditionally perked up when the hot-weather months rolled around, was about to fall into a six-week stretch of doldrums which he would alternately attribute to shoulder tendonitis and back discomforts; but some observers openly wondered if the "old man"—skeptics still questioned his age—had finally extracted the last remaining miles from that overpowering right arm. No one, including Luis, bothered to suggest that the mental strain of his parents' plight might have been taking the biggest toll of all.

On July 4 Luis hurled a four-hitter at the Indians and lost, 4–3, then won his twelfth game at home against the Rangers in a circus atmosphere. A crowd of more than 20,000 faithful sat through rain delays of 33 and 37 minutes and was amply rewarded by two exciting moments at the plate: Rice smashed his sixteenth homer somewhere into the distant overcast, and Tiant came to bat, making him the first Boston pitcher to go to the plate in three years, thanks to the advent of the designated hitter. Cecil Cooper had opened the game in the DH spot, but when he was sent out to play first base after Yastrzemski was pulled out of the lineup, the rules dictated that Tiant had to assume his own batting responsibilities. Wearing a warm-up jacket and swinging a weighted bat, Luis strode to the plate like a reincarnation of the Babe himself as both dugouts came to attention. "I'm going to go long," he predicted to Burleson, who promptly agreed to a bet. A roar went up from the stands as Luis stroked a fly to deep right field. It was caught, but he wore a smile as he jogged back to the bench and headed straight for the little shortstop whom he had nicknamed "The Rooster." "Let's have the dollar," he demanded.

He won his next outing, too, beating Kansas City in a torrid Boston heat wave, 8–3, but then dropped a pair to Texas and New York in which he gave up 21 hits in 13 innings.

His record for July had been 2–3, leaving him 13–10 on the season.

On August 1 the temperature in Fenway Park at 7:30 P.M. was 100 degrees, but more than 26,000 fans turned out to watch Luis take on the Tigers and, more important, to cheer the streaking Red Sox, who were rapidly pulling away from second-place Baltimore. Tiant had missed his last scheduled turn because of shoulder miseries, and once again this night it was obvious he was still having problems. Detroit got 14 hits off of him, including Willie Horton's game-tying, three-run homer in the ninth, but Yastrzemski and Doyle each singled in the tenth to provide the winning run which enabled Boston to keep its 8½-game advantage. Luis wasn't around, however; the victory went to reliever Jim Willoughby.

On August 5 he lost his fourth decision in a row, bowing to Baltimore, 3–0, before a jammed crowd at Fenway. But this wasn't going to be Boston's night in any event, for Jim Palmer was brilliant in holding the Red Sox to two scratch singles while posting his sixteenth win, tops in the majors.

With a 7½-game lead and Earl Weaver's warnings about looking over their shoulders, the Sox took off for a grinding 15-game road trip that would carry them across the country and back.

Luis went seven innings in Oakland and beat the A's for the fifth consecutive time, 5–3, but five hits and two walks indicated he was still struggling. A 430-foot homer by Rice helped his cause, along with relief from the dependable Boston bullpen, which had recorded 21 saves in five weeks.

Five days later he pitched his first complete game in a month, beating Chicago, 3–2, on a tidy though unspectacular seven-hitter. The Red Sox had flown him into the Windy City ahead of his teammates, hoping the early arrival would provide extra rest for his shoulder along with combating jet lag. Though the club was doing well on the trip, maintaining a comfortable lead over the Orioles, there was continued anxiety over Tiant's failure to regain his commanding form. If Baltimore should rise up and make a fight of it down the homestretch—and no one in Boston was foolish enough to dismiss that possibility—a healthy Tiant would be invaluable; indeed, perhaps even indispensable. "The shoulder feels better," Luis insisted after the game. "I'm starting to get the ball where I want it again."

But on Wednesday, August 20, he gave up nine hits and struck out none as Kansas City beat him, 3–1. *C'est la vie!* On this particular night the loss seemed incidental. The Sox had finished their grueling cross-country grind with a very satisfying 9–6 mark. They were content.

And Luis? While he was trying to concentrate on getting the Royals out, his parents were sitting in the U. S. Embassy office in Mexico City, waiting for the final visa clearance that would enable them to fly to Boston for what Luis had correctly anticipated would be "the greatest day of my life."

CHAPTER 27

Reunited at Last

The Red Sox entourage arrived at Logan International Airport late that night, and Luis headed straight for Milton.

"I wondered what he would be like," Maria says. "If he would be nervous, or excited, or upset. I know I was a little bit nervous. But he seemed so calm, like nothing was bothering him. And that night he had a good sleep."

Of course he had had almost four months to prepare for the moment he had awaited for almost 15 years, and he had been in telephone contact with his parents prior to their departure from Havana. But there's really no way to prepare one's emotions, at least not the same way travel plans and accommodations can be prepared with casual perfunctoriness. What do you say? What do you do? How do you begin? He didn't know.

"I wondered what my father would look like," he remembers. "And my mother, too. I told myself that they would look older, so I wouldn't be surprised."

For 12-year-old Luis, seven-year-old Isabel and one-year-old Danny, it would be their very first meeting with their grandfather, and for Maria the first time she met the man who had been her father-in-law for the past 14 years.

Reporters besieged the Milton home with interview requests, but Luis carefully avoided them. "I tried to hide," he explains, "because I knew my parents would be tired and I didn't want a lot of confusion and excitement at the airport."

At last the time came to climb into the car and begin the 10-mile trip up the Southeast Expressway, through the Callahan Tunnel, and into Logan's sprawling network of terminals and garages, home of the eighth busiest airport in the world. Luis wheeled the big Cadillac into a nearby parking facility, then quietly led his family through the maze of baggage counters, information desks, refreshment stands and ticket windows, over to the escalator that brought them up to the American Airlines waiting room. As Luis turned the corner to enter the room, he was horrified.

"It seemed like every sportswriter and cameraman in the world was there," he recalls. "They all came rushing over to take pictures and ask questions. I could understand why they were there, but it still upset me. I wanted to be alone right then."

The famous Tiant coolness remained intact, however, as he tried to co-operate without inviting a massive barrage of requests and inquiries.

Then an announcement pierced the air, directing everyone's attention to the terminal gate where the huge silver carrier was just pulling in. Instinctively, the media crowd stepped back a bit, allowing Luis, Maria and the children enough room for the imminent reception to take place.

Luis reached into his pocket and took out a clean white handkerchief. He quickly dabbed his brow. And waited.

"As soon as I saw my father step off of that plane, I put my hands over my eyes and cried," he remembers. "I wasn't going to do that, but I couldn't help it."

Señor Tiant immediately spotted his son and broke into a wide smile as Luis rushed to embrace him.

"Don't cry," his father whispered. "The cameras will see you."

"I don't care," Luis said, hugging him harder. "That's the way I feel."

The old man closed his eyes a moment, then turned to meet the rest of his family.

Maria kissed him, then one by one the children did, too, while Luis held his mother.

In the mob of reporters and photographers there were very few dry eyes.

After an appropriate interlude a writer ventured forward, accompanied by a Spanish interpreter.

Mrs. Tiant was asked if her husband was prepared to pitch for the Red Sox, if needed. "I don't know," she said. "It's been so long since he threw a ball. He'd have to go into training."

Señor Tiant eavesdropped, then interrupted. "She doesn't understand baseball," he grinned. "You tell the Red Sox I'm ready."

Then he looked at little Luis again and said to a reporter, "He's going to make a great ballplayer."

Finally Luis slipped an arm around his father's waist.

"Come on," he said, "let's all go home."

On TV screens throughout New England that night the Tiant story was treated as top news, dramatically captured on film. Cecil Cooper's wife cried as they watched it. So did Jim Rice's. So did a lot of other people—friends and strangers alike—who came up to Luis in following days and simply expressed their joy and best wishes. More than his many big victories, it seemed, this had been a chapter of his life that everyone felt like applauding.

That night the Tiants had a lot to talk about, a lot to ask, a lot to tell and a lot to remember. Luis and his father had a few drinks, a few cigars and more than a few laughs. So much had been pent up for so long, and now it began to pour forth in a relentless stream of conversation as the father and the son renewed their bonds into the wee hours of another day.

But Señora Tiant was very tired. The long trip and then the emotional reunion had clearly left her spent. Maria could see that right away, so she showed her mother-in-law to her room.

Before retiring, however, Luis' mother kissed her son good night.

"I'm so happy," she told him softly, eyes brimming, "I don't care if I die now."

CHAPTER 28

Divisional Champions

The Red Sox began their 11-game home stand by winning two out of three from Chicago. Then Tuesday night, August 26, Señor Tiant got his first opportunity to watch his son pitch.

As the Tiant family car approached Fenway Park, several hours before game time, its occupants were greeted by many signs of welcome, including a huge banner hung across a Kenmore Square pizzeria that read: "Welcome Tiant Family . . . Good Luck, Luis!"

It was only a prelude of what was to come.

The Red Sox had wanted to extend an official gretting to Señor Tiant, even to the point of conducting a special pregame ceremony, but yet they were reluctant to interfere with what was basically a family affair. So during the series with Chicago, publicist Bill Crowley called Luis aside.

"We'd like to have your father join you on the mound before Tuesday's game," he explained, "but we don't want you or anyone to think we're trying to capitalize on the situation. So we'll leave it up to you."

Luis' initial reaction was negative, but the more he thought about it, the more the scenario touched him. There wasn't a doubt in the world that his father belonged on a major league mound back in the days of his youth. But the times prohibited that, and now all that Señor Tiant could do was to live that dream vicariously through the accomplishments of his son. One artificial moment could never atone for all those tragically wasted years, but perhaps its symbolism would remind the world that Luis Tiant, Red Sox star, was the *second* great athlete in the family.

So Luis agreed.

Public-address announcer Sherm Feller began his introduction, citing "one of the greatest pitchers of the New York Cubans," but his words were drowned out as soon as the trim visitor, wearing a brown suit and a Red Sox cap, emerged from the Boston dugout, accompanied by his namesake, who was wearing uniform No. 23. As one, the crowd of 32,086 stood up and gave a tremendous ovation as the father and son made their way to the mound, a thrilling roar that was punctuated by shouts of "Loo-ie, Loo-ie!" It continued unabated until Señor Tiant removed his jacket and handed it to Luis, who stood beside him, covered with goosebumps.

Catcher Tim Blackwell flashed a signal, then the old man went into a full, graceful motion and fired a pitch—low and outside. He looked disapprovingly toward the plate, then called for the ball again. Once more he went into his windup and delivered—this time, *bringing in some heat,* right through the middle of the strike zone!

The fans were on their feet again in a rousing salute as he donned his jacket and headed back to the dugout.

"He told me he was ready to go four or five innings anytime," Luis grinned.

But now it was time to return to the pennant race.

Luis, to put it delicately, was clobbered, 8–2, and even the four errors his teammates committed behind him couldn't have changed what had been a very poor performance. His record was now 15–13.

"I'll tell you something," Crowley admits. "I can recall sitting in the press box that night and saying, 'It's too bad the old man arrived a year too late.' I kept wishing he could have been there a year earlier when Luis was really good. But now you couldn't help suspecting that maybe he had had it. It wasn't just me. A lot of people in the box that night were saying it."

And that fear was greatly reaffirmed four nights later when Luis started against the A's and was driven out of the game in less than three innings, yielding seven hits and three walks in that brief time.

Tommy Harper, who had been sold by the Angels to Oakland three weeks earlier, watched his friend's performance and was troubled.

"You know, Luis isn't a complainer," Tommy says, "but I knew his back was killing him. He could hardly bend over, so there was no way he could do the things he wanted to do with the ball. It was coming in high, and when Luis gets the ball high he's going to get killed. He knows that. And so does everybody else. I can remember Sal [Bando] coming back into the dugout in the first inning and telling us, 'He's not throwing today, guys.' Hitters can tell when a pitcher hasn't got his stuff, and it was obvious Luis didn't have anything out there."

Luis had been here before. The 1971 Twins, believing they had a shot at a third consecutive divisional crown (which they didn't), had no time for injured pitchers whose futures were tied up in question marks. For them, as Redskins coach George Allen would put it, "the future is now." And Luis, at best, was *later*. So they said goodbye and tossed him to the winds.

The Red Sox weren't disposed to dump him. Not at all. Nor were they ruling him out of their plans. But they were in the middle of a pennant race with an excellent shot at copping their first crown in eight years, so, reluctantly, they put him out of their minds for the time being.

"People say I'm a happy, funny guy, that I make all the players relax," Tiant muses. "But all of that doesn't mean a thing if you can't produce when your team sends you out there. I kidded with everybody in Minnesota and made a lot of friends, but as soon as they thought I couldn't win anymore, they told me they didn't want me. Being a nice guy wasn't important. You've got to be a winner. It's a business thing, and I understand it."

But it's also a personal thing, too.

"When you're going good everybody loves you," Luis points

out. "But as soon as I started having that back problem, I'd turn on the radio and hear people saying I was old and no good anymore. That really hurt me. But I had been through it and I knew how to take it."

Controlling the mind, he explains, is just as important as controlling a pitch.

"Sometimes you can't stop yourself from worrying," he explains. "We all have things that bother us. But what you have to do is keep believing in yourself, keeping trying your hardest, and keep having faith that God knows what He is doing. You can't let yourself give up, or get so nervous and upset that you stop performing. Whenever things go wrong for me, I keep reminding myself of these things because I know they're true."

Following the Oakland shelling, Luis remained on the sidelines for 10 days, missing two scheduled starts. He accompanied the club to Milwaukee in the first week of September, and while he was there he visited Dr. Gary Gutten, an orthopedic specialist, who took X rays of the problem area in his back. The results were all negative.

But the pains—spasms—persisted, and Luis was becoming distraught over the idea of possibly missing a chance to play in the World Series, even though he kept reassuring himself that time would heal his wounds. But was there enough time left?

One of Maria's closest friends in the neighborhood is a lady named June Elam, who happened, in the middle of her life, to get caught up in the macrobiotic movement, even to the point of traveling into Boston regularly to study under an oriental practitioner of acupressure and Shiatsu massages.

"It's really the study of long life," she explains. "We don't believe in filling up bodies with pills and medicines. We study the diets used by the Zen Buddhist monks who were known for their long life spans. To people who don't understand this, it sounds like a lot of witchcraft or something like that. But we're really not crazy. We're simply trying to get back to a tradition that people had thousands of years ago in the Orient when they were very spiritual and liked to live in harmony with the universe."

Which brings us to Luis, whose immediate interest was getting back into harmony with the American League East.

Richard Elam, June's 13-year-old son, was visiting his friend young Luis one day when heard Maria talking about Luis' aching back. When June stopped by later in the day, Richard suggested, "Ma, why don't you tell Maria how you fix people's backs?"

Maria looked up, June shrugged, and soon they were deep into discussing Shiatsu massages and such. When Luis returned home, Maria told him about her conversation with June. Whether he believed in the theories or not was quite beside the point; the whole country was keyed up for baseball and here he was, moping around Milton with a bum back.

What could he lose?

The answer, it turned out, was sleep.

"According to the Chinese clock," Mrs. Elam explains, "if you're treating an area where the pain is near the liver, for instance, then you massage at one o'clock in the morning. There are two hours every day when each organ responds better to a massage. If you massage at the right time, it gives the whole body a boost."

Luis' time, it seemed, was betweeen 1 A.M. and 3 A.M.

In addition to the massages, she also treated his back with ginger root compresses.

"You grate enough ginger root to make a pile the size of a golf ball," she instructed. "Then you wrap it into cheesecloth and dip it into a pot of water with the exact temperature of 158 degrees. If the water is any hotter than that you've ruined your preparation. You let it steep for three or four minutes, then press the cheesecloth against the side of the pot with a spoon or spatula until all of the juices come out into the water. Then you just dip towels into the water and press them against the sore areas. This gets the circulation going."

Luis also found himself becoming a Bancha tea drinker.

"The Tiants love to have company," June says. "Eventually someone would open up a wine bottle and ask Luis if he wanted a drink. He'd reach for the glass, but I'd take it away from him and give him a cup of Bancha tea instead. It's the only tea on the market that doesn't have carcinogen dye in it. A cup of that was in keeping with the rest of his treatments. It would give him a good night's sleep and keep his circulation flowing beautifully, because all of heaven's force would be co-operating with him."

There was no charge for her services, June explains.

"I didn't do it professionally. I did it out of love, because the Tiants are friends and neighbors of mine and I wanted Luis to be the best pitcher in the world."

So did Dick O'Connell, Darrell Johnson and a lot of other people.

In between ginger root compresses, Shiatsu massages and cups of Bancha tea, Luis also visited the Dorchester offices of Dr. Nathan Shapiro, a highly respected Boston physician well known for his service to the State Boxing Commission. Dr. Shapiro was also the father of Elaine Scheiber, Buddy's wife, which is how Luis happened to cross paths with him.

He conducted a series of X-ray tests on Tiant's left sacroiliac region and discovered an inflammation at the joint of the pelvis and spine. He immediately began ultrasonic treatments, along with prescribing therapeutic exercises. Several days later he shot more pictures.

"By showing Luis the before and the after shots, he could see for himself what was taking place," Dr. Shapiro says. "And seeing is believing. I assured him he'd soon be feeling 100 per cent, and I think he needed that more than anything else."

On Thursday afternoon, September 11, Luis was pronounced ready for action. Darrell Johnson didn't waste any time finding out the answer to the question on everyone's mind. He penciled Luis in as his starting pitcher against Detroit that same afternoon.

If Tiant was going to be a factor the rest of the way, now was the time for him to show it.

The Sox scored twice in the second inning to provide him with a bit of a cushion. Everything was working for the mustachioed maestro, it seemed. He was twisting and turning and at his herky-jerky best, throwing from all angles and at all speeds as the Tigers stood stunned at the plate wondering what in hell was going on out there. They were seeing what could only be described as *pure* Tiant, Luis in his very finest form, in complete control of the game and loving every minute of it. At the end of six innings Detroit hadn't even come close to getting a base hit. After seven innings the aura of an impending no-hitter had Fenway fans in knots. Then there was one out in the eighth. Now two outs in the eighth—and still no Tiger hits! Aurelio Rodriguez came to bat and worked the count to three-and-two. Then he reached out and tapped Luis' next offering over second base for a scratch single that raised his batting average to a lusty .250.

"Don't talk about a lucky hit," Señor Tiant admonished a writer in the locker room. "The man hit the ball pretty good."

As soon as the cluster of writers backed off, he walked over to Luis' locker and clamped his son in a hearty embrace before both of them posed behind a pair of rich Havana cigars.

Luis had wound up with a three-hitter, striking out 10, in what was surely his best performance of the year.

It had been a "Loo-ie, Loo-ie!" ball game from start to finish.

Luis' mother is not an outwardly emotional lady, but the thrill of watching the noisy Fenway crowd cheering and swaying with his every pitch, shouting his praises, moved her deeply.

"This is all I want out of life," she told Marta DeCelle as they waited for Luis to come out of the locker room. "He is all we have, and all that's important to me is that happiness and goodness come to him."

"It was so beautifully said," Marta recalls. "She brought tears to my eyes."

By now the city of Boston—where one can read baseball columns in January!—was in an absolute Red Sox frenzy. The Orioles had crept to within 4½ games, and a Baltimore disc jockey had taken an autographed Red Sox baseball to Nairobi, where a witch doctor had supposedly wrapped it in human hairs and then chanted incantations over it! Crazy, right? No, crazy, wrong. It was the hottest topic in town.

And here were those damned Orioles arriving at Fenway for two games, two games that could bring them perilously close to first place. Tickets to the games? You had a better chance of getting a private audience with the Pope.

Perhaps Bostonians didn't *really* believe in Nairobi witch doctors, but they sure as hell believed in the Orioles. Just a year ago the O's trailed the Red Sox by eight games on August 29, and wound up seven games ahead of Boston when the final gun sounded. Damned right they believed in the Orioles! And Earl Weaver, their mischievous manager, reminded Boston writers upon his arrival in town: "We've crawled out of more coffins than Bela Lugosi!"

There was never any doubt about Darrell Johnson's pitching choice for Game 1 of the critical two-game set.

The moment the bullpen gate swung open, 15 minutes before game time, almost 35,000 voices began to scream in unison: "Loo-ie, Loo-ie, Loo-ie!"

"I've always said, if I had to pick one guy to pitch a game I wanted to win, it would be Tiant," Yastrzemski says.

"When he's pitching," Rico Petrocelli adds, "I just feel we're going to win."

Two zany Boston fans, absurdly garbed in what they perceived to be the latest in witch doctor fashions, climbed upon the Baltimore dugout roof and began to dance to the rhythm of 35,000 bravos.

It was Fenway Park in its quintessence.

And it got what it deserved: the quintessential Tiant show!

He struck out eight, gave up five meaningless hits, and held the Baltimore batters in the palm of his hand all night.

Lee May struck out three times, once with men on second and third. "He was making unbelievable pitches to me. He almost had me walking across the plate trying to reach them!"

The 2–0 victory was Luis' first shutout of the season, his seventeenth win of the year. It was also the nail in a coffin that even Bela Lugosi couldn't have opened, for the Orioles now trailed by 5½ games with only a dozen to go.

"You can talk about anybody else on that team you want to," said losing pitcher Jim Palmer (20–11), "but Tiant is *The Man.*"

"Voodoos and spells are okay," Ray Fitzgerald wrote in the *Globe,* "but when the chips are on the line, give me Luis Tiant, doing a 90-degree turn and humming the ball on the outside corner for a called strike three."

Later that night Red Sox officials announced details for the sale of playoff tickets.

The playoffs!

That's all Luis had thought about while waiting for his back to heal. "I don't know how many years I have left," he said that night, "and one thing I really want to do before I'm done is pitch in the World Series."

The playoffs!

That's why Yastrzemski rejected a doctor's suggestion that he take a short rest after sustaining a slight shoulder separation in early August. "Maybe I should have taken some time off," he conceded, "but all I want to do is help this team win a damned pennant. That's what it's all about. Period. And when you get this close, you want it so badly that you just can't imagine not playing every day."

It was all over but the shouting—and there was plenty of that —as Luis walked out to the mound in a pea soup fog on Friday evening, September 26, to work the first game of a doubleheader against the Indians. The magic number was 2. A sweep tonight and Boston would clinch a tie for first. It was never close. He threw a four-hit shutout at his former team, and then oft-maligned Reggie Cleveland came on to throw a five-hit shutout in the nightcap!

On Saturday it became official: The Red Sox were the 1975 champions in the American League East.

With three remarkable performances in September, Luis was now ready to show the world what the patrons of Fenway Park already knew: *He was the best damned pitcher in baseball!*

PART VI
A World Series Hero

CHAPTER 29

A Pennant Flies in Boston

Strange things can happen in so short a series, but no one is better equipped to deal with things strange than the feisty young men from Oakland. Expect Boston to suffer their wrath.

—*Sports Illustrated*

That was not idle speculation or a throwaway line to help complete a story. On the contrary, the general consensus seemed to be that experience would prove the difference. After all, Oakland had won its fifth American League West championship in a row and was now looking for its fourth consecutive world championship as well.

And the Red Sox? They had been 1967 pennant winners. Period.

"Want to hear something funny?" Rico Petrocelli smiled as he sat in front of his locker on the eve of the playoff opener. "I spent that whole winter just wondering who we'd be playing in the 1968 World Series. That sounds crazy now, doesn't it?"

Not really. The 1967 Sox had good reason to be thinking that way. They were young and talented and seemingly "Destiny's Darlings," as an adoring Boston press was wont to call them that year. But now, as literally hundreds of media soldiers converged on Fenway Park to report on the 1975 playoffs, there were reminders of that unfulfilled dream. Tony Conigliaro, the local boy who led the league in homers at the age of 20 and then suffered a near-fatal beaning two years later in August of 1967, was now carrying a microphone for WJAR-TV in Providence, interviewing Yastrzemski. Despite two courageous comeback attempts, the most recent in the spring of 1975, Tony was never able to recapture the good times. Jim Lonborg, the handsome 22-game winner whom fans carried off the field on their shoulders after that final-day victory in 1967, badly injured his knee in a skiing mishap that winter and never regained his championship form. Lonnie was now in town to provide color commentary on the playoff telecasts. Ken Harrelson, the flamboyant "Hawk" who arrived in 1967, led the Sox in homers and RBI in 1968 and was then traded away in 1969, touching off the most angry fan reaction in Boston since the Bruins sold Tiny Thompson, the Hall of Fame goalie, 30 years earlier, was doing television work for the team now.

Rico spotted them in the crowded locker room and waved.

"Just looking at them brings back so many memories," the 32-year-old veteran said. "We were like little kids in 1967, jumping around in the dugout, acting giddy, having fun every day. Winning seemed so natural then. I guess it's always that way when you're young. And we were winning all the time, it seemed. Fans were coming and reporters were asking questions and people were stopping us on the streets to talk baseball and congratulate us. It was beautiful. And I guess I thought it would never end."

He laughed softly, almost as if he was mocking himself.

"But I'm older now," he sighed, "and I know better than that."

The 1967 Red Sox held the future in their hands, then watched as it slipped through their fingers. And now only Rico and Yaz remained.

The 1971 Oakland A's, by contrast, grabbed the future and never let go. They were perhaps the most raucous, uninhibited champions baseball had seen since St. Louis spawned its Gashouse Gang more than a generation earlier. But on the field, where the only antics that counted took place, the A's played baseball like the Swiss make watches. They were clean and precise and awfully, awfully good.

And so the image of lambs being led to slaughter was not without foundation.

But the Red Sox, though undeniably still wet behind the ears, had proven their mettle this season, too. Thirty of their 95 victories, for instance, had come after they entered the seventh inning either tied or trailing.

Ah, but that was during the regular schedule, the sages warned, and everybody knew the playoffs would be an entirely different proposition.

Petrocelli, by nature, is a quiet, introspective player, not usually given to clubhouse tomfoolery and such. But in the week leading up to Saturday's playoff opener against the A's, he began counseling his youthful teammates, unobtrusively, one by one, gradually getting his message across.

"The idea is to be aggressive," he said. "Go out there thinking you're going to do your best. Just keep thinking that, and all nervousness will go away. Don't be thinking it's Vida Blue or Rollie Fingers or anyone else out there on the mound. Just be watching the ball, not the man who throws it. And just keep telling yourself you're going to hit that damned thing. Same way in the field. Forget the guy at the plate. All you care about is catching the ball. If we just concentrate on baseball—nothing else—we can beat any team in the world."

Luis, however, needed no pep talks. There were no stars in his eyes, nor were there any butterflies in his stomach. He had survived too many crises in the past to be flighty over the prospect of facing Oakland in the playoffs. Besides, if he was at all concerned about the Athletics, *how in the world should they have felt about him?* He had beaten them five times in a row prior to that August 30 debacle, and that last episode was plainly attributable to his back miseries.

Tiant had no fear of Oakland.

And his performance proved it.

In four of the first six innings he retired the A's one-two-three. Only two walks in the third and a single in the fifth interrupted his total dominance. After Bill North led off the first by flying to center, both Claudell Washington and Sal Bando looked at called third strikes. Reggie Jackson opened the second with another fly to center, then Gene Tenace and Joe Rudi both looked at called third strikes!

"Loo-ie, Loo-ie, Loo-ie!" The multitudes were singing his praises already. Each twist, each dip, each violent jerk of the head was greeted with ooohs and aaahs as Tiant exhausted his spectacular repertoire of contortions and control.

"He's the Fred Astaire of baseball, dancing his way to victory," Jackson later marveled.

Meanwhile, the Sox grabbed an early 2–0 lead in the first on Yastrzemski's single up the middle and *three Oakland errors!* Golden Glover Rudi, normally the A's left fielder, had been shifted to first during the season. Washington, his replacement, was at best adequate in the field, and Fenway's left field has always been a notoriously poor spot for anyone plagued by uncertainty. Boston's first batter, Juan Beniquez, immediately made that point by lining a shot into left that Washington—in the words of the *Globe*'s Peter Gammons—"reacted to as if it were a phone ringing at 4:24 A.M." But he caught it for the first out. And when Denny Doyle grounded to second for a routine second out, it appeared that the A's were, indeed, their old invincible selves. Then Yaz hit his shot into center. And Fisk sent a hard chopper to the usually methodical Bando at third, but Sal misplayed the ball, allowing it to roll out to Washington, who then compounded the problem by throwing wildly back to Bando in an effort to cut down Yaz. Carl scored easily. And so did Fisk, moments later, when Lynn's grounder to Phil Garner at second was kicked away for error No. 3.

That was all Luis needed.

From the second through the sixth innings, Oakland starter Ken Holtzman set down 15 of the 18 batters he faced. The 2–0 margin remained unchanged.

Then the Sox teed off in the seventh. Doubles by Dwight Evans and Rick Burleson, singles by Beniquez, Fisk and Lynn, and a sacrifice fly by Doyle—all coming off a variety of three Oakland hurlers—propelled Boston into a 7–0 lead.

The only question now would be the icing on the cake: would Luis get his shutout?

Bert Campaneris opened the eighth with a grounder to short that Burleson booted. A double by pinch-hitter Jim Holt moved

Campy to third, and then Cooper's error on a North ground ball allowed him to score. That put runners on first and third with no outs, but Tiant remained unruffled as he eliminated both Washington and Bando on swinging third strikes and then got Jackson on an easy infield play. It was the third strikeout for Bando, who had been Oakland's hottest hitter throughout September.

As soon as Luis returned to the dugout, Burleson—easily the most intense competitor on the club—made a beeline for him and began blurting out an apology for his error. Luis just looked at him and smiled. "It's okay," he insisted, reassuring his young friend, "I know you were trying. We're going to win the game. That's all that matters to me. Don't let it bother you."

"That was nice of him," Rick said later. "I was really mad at myself. Maybe I was too keyed up; I don't know. But Luis was so calm. He made me feel a lot better."

The Oakland ninth was merely a formality. Tenace walked, but he was cut down on a fielder's choice after Rudi flied out. That brought up Campaneris with two outs.

"I went out onto the on-deck circle," Tommy Harper remembers. "If Campy reached base I was going to pinch-hit. The fans were going crazy, yelling 'Loo-ie, Loo-ie!' He got two strikes on Campaneris, then he sort of looked over to see who was due up next. When he saw me he started to smile. I pointed at myself, like I was saying, 'That's right, you've got to deal with me.' Luis laughed, then shook his finger at me, as if to say, 'No, no, you won't get the chance.'"

And Tommy didn't, for Campaneris lifted the next pitch high into the air, right over Petrocelli at third, and Rico put it away.

Thus ended an eight-strikeout three-hitter, Tiant's fourth consecutive victory at Fenway Park, all of which were vitally important games played in full view of a national spotlight. His ERA in those four games was a fabulous 0.25, and the triumph over the A's increased his stretch of consecutive innings without an earned run to 27!

But this particular win, beyond doubt, was the biggest single Red Sox win in eight years.

It belonged to a city that perennially produced one of the highest attendance figures in the majors, though its park had the next-to-lowest seating capacity in either league. And it belonged to a team that consistently silenced its detractors with crisp, alert performances all summer long.

But most of all, it belonged to one man.

"You saw a true professional out there today," Yaz advised. "What he's got is inside, and not many people have it. It's a gift and he makes the most of it."

He was talking, of course about *heart,* and if that sounded corny to the rest of the world, be assured it was no laughing matter in the Oakland locker room.

Alvin Dark, the same Alvin Dark who feuded with Luis over his pitching techniques in Cleveland, was now the Oakland manager, and he was facing a battery of writers in the main interview hall when Tiant arrived at the microphones.

"Luis," Alvin smiled, patting him on the head, "you were just beautiful out there today."

Later, in his office next to the visiting clubhouse, Dark raved about the man who handcuffed his champions.

"I'll bet this," Alvin said. "I'll bet as he goes through all of those movements, he still hasn't made up his mind just how he's going to throw the pitch. I think he starts out intending to throw it overhand, because that's most comfortable for him. Then all of a sudden he gets an idea. He'll decide sidearm might work better, or maybe he'll decide to throw three quarters for a change. Most pitchers type themselves. You watch them make a few throws and you can pretty well tell what kind of a game they're going to pitch. But Tiant is something else. I watched him throw real hard for two innings, so we talked about that on the bench. Then suddenly he changed. He began throwing to spots with all kinds of stuff. In all the time I managed him with the Indians I never knew which way he was going to throw the ball. And I don't know now, either."

Red Smith, the venerable New York *Times* columnist who's been chronicling professional sports for half a century, was no less enthralled than the ecstatic hometown audience. "He is a joy to watch, this swarthy, ample gentleman of 34 going on 44. Blackbearded and sinister, he looks like Pancho Villa after a tough week of looting and burning. . . . He is a master of every legal pitch, and he never throws two consecutive pitches at the same speed. . . . On his best day, he could not have been much better than he was [today]."

Though Tim Horgan probably said it best in the next day's Boston *Herald American:*

"El Tiante was, in a word, gorgeous as he sketched another of those jobs that belongs more in an art gallery than a ball yard."

The victory did a lot more for the Red Sox than simply providing them with a one-game edge in this best-of-five series. It shattered any aura the Athletics might have had in the minds of Boston's youthful stars. It reaffirmed Petrocelli's wise advice. It proved a very valid point. There's an engraved sign sitting on a shelf in the office of Boston Celtics president Red Auerbach, a little piece of memorabilia dating back to the days of the fabulous (11 titles in 13 years) dynasty. It reads: *"Experience Don't Mean Shit!"—Bill Russell, 1966.* And now the Red Sox had discovered that for themselves.

"From what I kept reading in the papers," Dwight Evans said, "I got the feeling we shouldn't have even bothered playing today. All I read and heard about was Oakland's experience. But we don't buy that. All it boils down to is our talents against their talents. We know we can beat them if we just play our games."

The next day the Sox went out and beat the A's again, 6–3, sparked by home runs from those two 1967 "Impossible Dreamers," Yastrzemski and Petrocelli.

Two nights later Rick Wise applied the *coup de grâce,* 5–3, in Oakland-Alameda County Coliseum.

And so the Red Sox were American League champions.

Now all that remained was a World Series, and everyone knew who would start for Boston in Game 1.

CHAPTER 30

Two-minute Curveballs

The Cincinnati Reds had won 108 games in the regular season, more than any other National League team since the 1909 Pirates, and their remarkable 64–17 record at Riverfront Stadium made them the winningest home team in National League history.

Suddenly, worrying about Baltimore and Oakland seemed like small matters compared to the threat now posed by this "Big Red Machine" that had been assembled on the banks of the Ohio.

Having swept past Pittsburgh in three playoff preliminaries, the Reds were now prohibitive favorites to beat Boston handily.

> We're like Rodney Dangerfield: We don't get no respect! Maybe because we're not a popoff club. We're just quietly confident. But the A's know how good we are. We beat them in every facet of this game, and—like the champions they are—they all said so when it was over. Personally I'm happy we're playing Cincinnati. They're the best, so they're the team we should be playing.—Rick Wise

The night before Game 1 there was the usual crowd of friends gathered at the Tiant home in Milton, laughing, sharing a few drinks, and talking about the upcoming game. Luis was too busy being the perfect host to fret over the things Johnny Bench, Pete Rose, Joe Morgan and Tony Perez might be planning to do to his pitches. When the last guest left and the lights were finally switched off, he slipped into bed.

It was 2 A.M.

"I slept like a baby," he remembers. "But just before I closed my eyes I thought about how this was something I had waited all my life for, and I thanked God my parents were going to be there to share it with me."

Nine Reds up and nine Reds down: that was the story of the first three innings as Luis breezed through the entire Cincinnati lineup without a hint of difficulty.

Then, with one out in the fourth, Joe Morgan singled and set the stage for Tiant's only crisis of the day. There had much been ado in the days leading up to the opener regarding Luis' motion. Cincinnati manager Sparky Anderson warned he would blow the whistle at the first sign of a balk. "I don't want to make a mockery or a farce out of the World Series," he explained, "but I've seen Tiant pitch. It isn't the way he flutters, bringing his hands down to his waist, that bothers me. It's the times when he stops his hands at the waist, and then drops them another notch before throwing to first. That's a balk as far as I'm concerned." Red Sox officials were indignant, claiming Luis had never been called for a balk in 11 years of major league pitching.

It was more than just pre-Series fodder to fill up news columns, for the Reds were the fastest team in their league, stealing 168 bases in 205 attempts. Luis' ability to keep them on first base loomed very important.

And now Morgan, the fastest Red of all with 68 steals in 78 tries, had reached first. Both dugouts came to attention.

"I was moving my feet and bending my knees, but I wasn't throwing to first," Luis later insisted. "He [National League umpire Nick Colosi] said I can't do that, so he called a balk. I ran over and asked him, 'How can that be a balk if I've pitched that way all my life?' He said it was, so I got mad."

So did more than 35,000 members of the Fenway Park jury who showered Colosi with boos and inquiries regarding his ancestry.

Tiant stomped back to the mound, got Bench on a pop-up to Fisk and then steered a called third strike past Perez to end the inning.

At about that time the Reds were ready to throw away their scouting reports.

"Our reports told us that 80 per cent of his pitches were fastballs," Rose said, shaking his head. "We even saw films of him blowing them past Bando and Jackson. So that's what we were looking for. I couldn't believe what I saw. We haven't got anybody in the National League like that, nobody who throws spinning high curveballs that take two minutes to come down!"

After 6½ innings the score was still 0–0.

Then the Sox unloaded with six runs in the seventh, beginning when Luis led off with a single to left. Evans then laid down a sacrifice that Reds pitcher Don Gullett threw into center field in his haste to cut down Tiant. When Denny Doyle followed with a single, Luis found himself standing on third.

"I asked him how he was doing," Rose reported later. "I don't know why I even bothered asking. All I had to do was look at the scoreboard."

Yaz kept the rally going with a single into right, and the crowd roared as Luis ambled in with the first run of the game. Or did he? Moments after crossing the plate he nonchalantly turned around and faced catcher Bench. Then he whirled into the plate, touching home to make his run official.

"I missed it the first time by half an inch," he sheepishly explained. "No one had to tell me. I knew I missed it. But I didn't want to hurry back. I wanted to go back easily, you know? I didn't want anybody to see me."

One person saw him quite clearly and couldn't wait to get him on the phone at game's end.

"Your swing is great, but don't ever get on base again or you're likely to get killed," Tommy Harper advised.

Singles by Fisk, Petrocelli and Burleson fueled the uprising until Luis had been furnished with his 6–0 cushion.

And everybody, including the Reds, realized that school was out.

Cincinnati went down in order in the eighth and ninth innings as Luis—cheered by repeated standing ovations—racked up his fifth key victory in a row, needing only 113 pitches to dismantle the "Big Red Machine." He had now gone 36 innings in Fenway Park without allowing an earned run.

"He has a style all his own," Rick Wise noted while literally hundreds of writers probed for the proper analysis of what they had just witnessed. "It's the same story every time he pitches. Besides throwing from five or six different angles, he's not afraid to throw off-speed when he falls behind on a count. That means hitters can't gear up for his fastball. And when they do see it, it ends up looking twice as fast because they aren't prepared for it. Luis is simply remarkable."

A few of the Reds apparently didn't agree, for writers arriving from their locker room brought the word that some Cincinnati batters plainly weren't impressed.

"Shit," Stan Williams smiled, "Luis doesn't want to impress them. He only wants to beat them."

In the midst of the postgame chaos, Luis received a message that Howard Cosell wanted him to catch the soonest shuttle possible and make a very lucrative appearance on his network variety show that night.

He declined, for he had other plans.

While the nation's presses churned out accolades in his behalf, Luis quietly entertained family and friends that evening in the Milton homestead. This had been his day of days. It needed no extra trimmings. All he wanted now was the company of friends and time for reflection.

Señor Tiant sat in a corner of the downstairs game room, alone with his thoughts, when Luis happened to walk by.

"He had been playing with the children for a while," Nick Trifone recalls, "and then he sort of sat there and watched all the people coming and going. I just happened to look over as Luis went by. The old man reached out and pulled him down onto his lap. He just looked at him for a minute and patted his arm and then began to cry. Luis did, too. There's no way of knowing how much the day had meant to both of them."

CHAPTER 31

Coolness in the Clutch

Cincinnati came up with two runs in the ninth to win Game 2 in Fenway Park, 3–2. Then it moved ahead in the Series by winning the first Riverfront Stadium engagement, 6–5. That contest was highlighted by one of the most controversial plays in Series history. Boston had fought back from an early 5–1 deficit to tie the game on Evans' two-run homer in the ninth, 5–5. Cesar Geronimo opened the home half of the tenth with a single, and Ed Armbrister attempted to advance him with a bunt that dropped in front of home plate. Carlton Fisk tried to field the ball, but wound up colliding with Armbrister. When Fisk finally broke free, he grabbed the ball and fired a desperate throw that ended up in center field as Geronimo and Armbrister pulled safely into third and second, respectively. The Sox screamed "interference!," but plate umpire Larry Barnett insisted it wasn't and allowed the runners to remain where they were. An intentional walk to Rose loaded the bases, and Morgan's single to center brought in Geronimo with the winning run.

So once again the Sox looked to Luis for their rescue. Another loss would all but end their hopes, giving the Reds a 3–1 lead with three games to go.

"I was staying with Luis at the Ramada Inn in Cincinnati," Felix Fernandez remembers, "and the place was really a nuthouse. Everybody was running around all nervous and excited, worrying about the game that night, but Luis just sat around relaxing. I couldn't believe his composure. He was sipping his coffee like he didn't have a care in the world. I said, 'What's the matter with you? Don't you have any nerves in there?' He laughed at me and said:

Ud tiene dos bolsillos en la vida. Uno para ganar y otro para las derrotas y ud dede llevarlos con dignidad.

"I've heard him say it many other times. It's one of his favorite expressions:

You come here with two pockets. One is the winning pocket and the other is the losing pocket and you have to carry the two pockets with dignity."

The Reds jumped on Tiant for two runs in the first inning, but when Boston broke loose for five in the fourth it seemed quite certain Luis had all the insurance he would need to begin bobbing and weaving and casting his magic once again. Give him room to breathe and he becomes unstoppable. Everyone understood that.

Except the Reds. With two outs in their half of the fourth, George Foster singled, Dave Concepcion doubled and Geronimo banged a triple. Luis prevented Cincinnati from tying the game by retiring pinch-hitter Terry Crowley on a swinging third strike, but Boston's lead had been slashed to one, 5–4, and there was still more than half a game to play.

Tiant gave the Reds two walks in the fifth.

He allowed a two-out bloop single in the sixth.

In the seventh he had a one-two-three inning.

All the Reds got in the eighth was a two-out single.

As Cincinnati came to bat in the bottom of the ninth, with a packed house of more than 55,000 partisans in an uproar, the score was still 5–4. The old bromide about the game not being over until the final out might draw snickers in some circles, but in

Cincinnati it's regarded as Gospel, and with good reason: During the regular season the Reds won 23 games in their final time at bat; they did it two more times in their playoff against the Pirates; and they did it in Games 2 and 3 of this Series!

"We never lose our cool," Joe Morgan says. "We always feel we can do what has to be done to win. And I was sure he couldn't shut us out for five innings in a row."

Geronimo opened with a single and was advanced to second when pinch-hitter Armbrister neatly sacrificed. Then Rose walked. Ken Griffey followed with a tremendous shot that traveled more than 400 feet into center, but Lynn made a spectacular over-the-shoulder catch.

Darrell Johnson walked out to the mound. Morgan waited at the plate, menacingly.

"What do you think?" the manager asked. "Have you got enough left?"

Luis smiled. "I've got him all the way."

Johnson nodded and returned to his dugout.

Moments later Morgan tapped out to Yaz at first, and the Red Sox had squared the Series at two games apiece, thereby guaranteeing a return to Fenway Park.

Luis had thrown 163 pitches, roughly 25 more than he does in a routine nine-inning game, and it was obvious he had been laboring most of the night. So reporters were quick to second-guess Johnson, demanding to know why he hadn't yanked Tiant with the dangerous Morgan due up.

"In a situation like that, when the chips are down, it's only once in a blue moon that Luis doesn't come through," he explained. "He's the man for a spot like that, and there was no way I was going to take him out unless he suggested it. He's done the job in the clutch all year long and I had every bit of faith in him tonight, even though it was the toughest one of all to pull out."

Peter Gammons had it right when he observed:

"In the game the Red Sox could not lose, El Tiante *would not lose!*"

CHAPTER 32

Beaten but Unbowed

If a man put a gun to my head and said I'm going to pull the trigger if you lose this game, I'd want Luis Tiant to pitch that game.
—*Darrell Johnson*

Tiant couldn't guarantee excellence every time. That was rather obvious in the cliff-hanger at Cincinnati if anyone really needed proof of the man's fallibility.

"But Luis doesn't have to have his good stuff to be able to go out and pitch a hell of a game," Yastrzemski points out. "With all of his angles and herky-jerkiness, he can get away with not having a good fastball or even a good breaking ball. Most pitchers must have their good stuff to pitch a good game. That's why I'd pick Luis if there was one game I had to win. He doesn't have to have everything going for him in order to win."

On Tuesday night, October 21, the Red Sox faced a game they *had* to win. Cincinnati won the final Riverfront Stadium encounter, 6–2, to take a 3–2 Series lead. Games 6 and 7 were scheduled for Boston, but it was fairly obvious there'd be no Game 7 if the Sox didn't prevail in Game 6 tonight.

That's the point an irate Bill Lee tried to make with Johnson when it was announced that Luis would work Game 6. Bill had originally been scheduled to pitch that one.

"Darrell told me he wanted to go with Luis because he felt Luis was the best," Lee says. "But I wanted to pitch again, and I felt I'd earned the chance. So I went into his office and told him: 'Tiant is not the best right now; he needs the rest. Let me throw the sixth game. We've got to win them both anyway, and you have to have confidence in me, too.' "

Johnson shook his head. His decision was firm. Luis would pitch the crucial sixth game.

"I'll tell you why that was," Lee said. "If I had pitched that game and lost, they'd have carried Darrell out of town on a rail. But if Luis pitched and lost, it would have been different."

Lee is probably right, for Luis had come to be regarded as the Savior at Fenway Park. Like high school cheerleaders chant: "If he can't do it, no one can!" That's how Boston felt about Tiant.

In the frantic closing weeks of September he had beaten the Tigers, 3–1; the Orioles, 2–0; and the Indians, 4–0; in the American League playoffs he had beaten the Athletics, 7–1; and so far in the Series he had beaten the Reds twice, 6–0 and 5–4.

Could he do it *just one more time?*

For a while it seemed so. Freddy Lynn hit a three-run homer in the first after Luis had retired the Reds with only a walk in the top half. In the second he got them one-two-three. In the third he yielded a two-out single to Rose. He allowed another two-out single to Perez in the fourth, but still he seemed to be safely in control of the situation.

Then in the fifth the Reds got to him. A walk, a single, a triple by Griffey, and a single by Bench evened the score at 3–3.

It remained that way through six innings, though Luis gave up two more hits.

Two singles and a George Foster double gave the Reds a 5–3 lead in the seventh.

When Geronimo led off the eighth with a homer into the right-field seats, putting Cincinnati ahead by a 6–3 count, Johnson finally emerged and removed Luis from the game. He had allowed 11 hits and six earned runs, but as he slowly retreated to the first base dugout the overflow crowd rose and swooned "Loo-ie, Loo-ie,

Loo-ie!" for the final time, sending him away with a gracious and heartfelt thank you.

For a man who had been rejected so often in the past, it was a moment to be cherished, because there was no mistaking what the fans were trying to tell him. It was a *beau geste* he'd always remember.

In one of the most dramatic, improbable chapters of World Series history, the Red Sox went on to win the game in 12 innings. Bernie Carbo got them back into it with a game-tying, three-run, pinch-hit homer after two were out in the eighth. Dewey Evans kept them in it in the eleventh with a one-handed catch of Morgan's shot to deep right, which he immediately fired back to first for a double play. And then Pudge Fisk, stealing a page from Bobby Thomson and Bill Mazeroski, cracked the game-winning homer in the bottom of the twelfth.

"I'll tell you something," Rose said afterward. "If anyone wants to sell the game of baseball, tonight's game is the one they should use."

But alas, Cincinnati prevailed in the seventh and final game, though it took Joe Morgan's RBI single in the ninth to squeeze past Boston, 4–3, thereby bringing to a close one of the tightest, best-played Series of all time.

"We were the better team," Sparky Anderson said, "but not by much."

Indeed, few heads were bowed in Boston's dressing room.

Petrocelli was near tears, but he spoke with pride. "People can say Cincinnati is great, but they damn well have to respect us, too. From September 1 through tonight we've played the most exciting baseball I've known in 11 years up here, and all of it with pressure and tension facing us night after night. Every game was like a World Series, and I'm so proud of this club tonight. These kids showed they have what it takes to be champions."

CHAPTER 33

Reflections

The 1975 World Series was viewed by more people around the world than any other Series in history.

And some of those people had a very special rooting interest.

"We were all pulling for him in Cleveland," says Cy Buynak, the Indians equipment manager. "Everybody who knew Luis when he was here just loved the guy. He was so super to all of us."

Up in Minnesota the television set in Dr. Harvey O'Phelan's home was tuned in, too.

"Yes, I'm surprised to see how far Luis has come back," says the man who treated the fateful 1970 injury. "And I'm also personally delighted. I just think the world of this fellow. Every contact I ever had with Luis was superb. He's a wonderful person."

But Luis found out a long time ago that friendships, popularity and past performances don't amount to a thing in terms of tomorrow. And so he probably wasn't at all shocked to discover that one of the first questions arising from the Series was: *How much longer can Tiant go on?* Indeed, there are knowledgeable people in Boston who'll insist his 1975 heroics occurred on borrowed time.

He first heard that in the fifties in Cuba.

It was still being said in the sixties in Cleveland.

So why should the seventies in Boston be any different?

"They're going to have to drag me out of this game," he smiles. "They tried it once and I came back. If they do it again, I'll keep coming back. When I first came to the Red Sox the pitching coach was Harvey Haddix. He told me he quit baseball because it stopped being fun for him. He said when that happens you have to quit or else the game will drive you crazy. I think he was right. But it's not my time to quit yet. Baseball is still fun for me."

"He's the toughest competitor I ever saw," Darrell Johnson insists. "I'm sure that's what kept him going when everything looked so bad a few years back. He tries so hard. I can see it every time he walks out to the mound. He thrives on competition. It's the competitive nature that first brings these men into sports, and as long as it remains they try to keep going.

"Sure, as you get older there are some things you find you can't do as well. But experience compensates for that quite often. Experience is just knowing what to do with what you've got. All the good pitchers I've ever seen—Koufax, Ford and so on—changed as time went on. They found ways to compensate. Luis does that, too. Yet he's still got all the pitches and all the moves, and he's still so damned deceptive.

"But the main thing I notice about Luis is that he still gets thrilled by winning. That tells me the man still loves this game."

One day late in September 1975, Luis drove into Boston with Nick Trifone. The stereo was playing and neither man spoke for miles.

Suddenly, Luis broke the silence. "You know, Nicky," he said, looking straight ahead as he drove, "I'm a lucky guy. All your life you wait for something, and now everything's coming up flowers."

It seemed that way to Luis as he sat in his backyard one afternoon just prior to the playoffs against Oakland. The kids were playing, his parents were sitting nearby and Maria was puttering around in her kitchen.

He turned to Felix Fernandez, his good friend.

Yo he senado muchas veces con una casa elegante con mis padres, mi esposa y mis hijos jugando en un patio grande; Yo nunca crei que esos suenos se convirtieran en realidad.

Then he leaned back in his chair and closed his eyes.

I have dreamed many times of having a beautiful home with my parents, my wife, and my children playing in a large playground; I never believed those dreams would come true.

But in 1975 they did. All his dreams came true.